DATE		

Gandhi
Today

Gandhi

Simple Productions
Arcata, California

Today

A REPORT ON MAHATMA GANDHI'S SUCCESSORS

by
Mark Shepard

Copyediting, design, production: Zipporah W. Collins, Berkeley, California
Proofreading: Mu'frida Bell, Berkeley, California
Typesetting: Pioneer Graphics, Eureka, California
Printing and binding: Edwards Brothers, Ann Arbor, Michigan

This book was word processed and coded on a Leading Edge Model D with
PC-Write, a shareware program ($16 with abridged manual from Quicksoft,
219 First N. #224, Seattle, Washington 98109). The book was set in Goudy
Oldstyle with Schneidler Black Italic display type.

Library of Congress Cataloging-in-Publication Data (Suggested)

Shepard, Mark, 1950–
  Gandhi today: a report on Mahatma Gandhi's successors.

  Bibliography: p. 134
  Includes index.
  1. Social change—Case studies. 2. Nonviolence.
3. Community development—India—Case studies. 4. Gandhi, Mahatma,
1869–1948—Political and social views. 5. India—Economic conditions—
1947– . 6. India—Social conditions—1947– . 7. Vinoba—1895–1982.
8. Narain, Jai Prakash. 9. Sarvodaya Movement (India). I. Title.
HN683.5.S54   1987   303.4'0954   86-61027
ISBN 0-938497-04-9
ISBN 0-938497-05-7 (pbk.)

Printed on acid-free paper

Manufactured in the United States of America

10 9 8 7 6 5 4 3 2

Simple Productions
12 East 15th Street, #3
Arcata, California 95521   USA

Contents

Foreword

Arun Gandhi ►

There are many who are now asking the question: Is Gandhi relevant today? Can his philosophy succeed?

This is tantamount to asking, Can love for humanity be relevant, or possible, today?—for Gandhi's philosophy is based on love, understanding, compassion for humankind.

Gandhi titled his autobiography *The Story of My Experiments with Truth*. Indeed, he treated his entire life as an experiment and expected his followers to carry on with this experiment after his death.

Mark Shepard is young, his mind is fresh, and his outlook robust enough to encompass new insights and pragmatic applications of the philosophy of love.

Arun Gandhi—a grandson of Mahatma Gandhi—is an internationally published journalist and a best-selling political writer in India. He currently edits and publishes a weekly newspaper in Bombay and is also engaged in an economic development project assisting villages south of the city.

A Note on Terms

Gandhi called his method of political action *Satyagraha*—a word he devised from two others and translated into English roughly as "soul-force" or "Truth-force." A more exact rendering might be "the force that is generated through adherence to Truth."

Outside India today, this method of Gandhi's is popularly called *nonviolence*. But Gandhi had a different use and meaning for the English word *nonviolence*, and the word he translated it from was different: *ahimsa*. This Hindu term normally means "a way of acting that refrains from hurting others." For Gandhi it came to mean a way of life based on love or compassion for all.

To Gandhi, then, Satyagraha was not the same as nonviolence but an outgrowth of it. In this book, Gandhi's distinction between the two concepts is preserved.

For Western readers, though, *Satyagraha* is too exotic a term for regular use. Other attempted substitutes over the years have included *passive resistance*—a term Gandhi used at first, then rejected—*nonviolent resistance, nonviolent direct action, nonviolent action*, and, most recently, *active nonviolence*. Following chapter 1, this book uses *nonviolent action* throughout.

But the equivalence of this substitute, as of the others, is only rough. *Nonviolent action*—in this book as elsewhere—can refer to any aggressive, purposeful action that refrains from physically harming the opponent. But, as chapter 1 describes, the *type* of nonviolent action that is Satyagraha goes much farther toward embodying nonviolence in Gandhi's sense.

Acknowledgments

My deep thanks to all who helped in this extensive enterprise; and my apologies to any I have failed to mention.

In India, thanks to my subjects: Chandi Prasad Bhatt, Narayan Desai, Radhakrishna and Nirmala Menon, Harivallabh Parikh, Prem Bhai and Dr. Ragini Prem, and Rama Shanker Bhai. To my hosts, advisers, and companions: A. B. and Rani Bhardwaj, Lok Sevak Sangh, M. Manickam, Daniel Mazgaonkar, K. Krishnan Nair, K. V. Parmar, Chris Sadler, Anne Marie de Witte. And to Gaje Singh Negi.

Special thanks for invaluable guidance and practical help to the Gandhi Peace Foundation and its staff, including: Radhakrishna, Mahendra Agrawal, T. S. Ananthu, Yogesh Kumar, Anupam Mishra, K. K. Mukherjee, Shalini Reyes, Rita Roy, Y. C. Sharma, Shobha, and N. Vasudevan.

In the West, to my agents: Hank Maiden and Michael Larsen. To my manuscript readers and consultants: Roderick Church, Kathy Dinaburg, Chuck Fager, Charles Fracchia, Daniel Halperin, Dan Hirsch, Alan Hoskins, Scott Kennedy, Erica and John Linton, Laura Magnani and Eric Moon, Lewis Michaelson, Geoffrey Ostergaard. To contributors toward my research expenses: Basileia House, Bruce and Ena Gurenson, Pam Weir. To several important moral supporters: Virginia Baron, Gene Knudsen-Hoffman, Shrikumar Poddar. And to those who offered comments for use in promotion, whose names appear elsewhere.

Thanks to all who took part in the publication of this book, whose names or businesses should be found listed elsewhere. Special thanks to Zipporah Collins for handling the book's incarnation with such marvelous effect.

Special thanks also to Charles Gurenson for his invaluable contribution.

Above all, thanks to Lillian Gurenson, my mother, friend, and partner, whose unfailing, selfless support made this book possible.

◂ *Mark Shepard*

Credits

Portions of this book in earlier versions have been published as follows:

Chapter 1
"Mahatma Gandhi: The Legacy," *Gandhi Marg* (221 Deen Dayal Upadhyaya Marg, New Delhi 110 002, India), April 1980.

Chapter 2
"Gandhi's Heirs," *WIN* (no longer publishing; 326 Livingston St., Brooklyn, New York 11217), June 1983; and *Shalom News* (Shalom House, 2100 North 13th St., Kansas City, Kansas 66104), December 1983.
An expanded version of this chapter was published as *Since Gandhi: India's Sarvodaya Movement*, Greenleaf Books, Weare, New Hampshire 03281, 1983.

Chapter 3
"Shanti Sena," *Peace News* (8 Elm Ave., Nottingham, England), May 26, 1981; and *Peacemaker* (P.O. Box 627, Garberville, California 95440), September 1981.
"Aggressive Peacemaking" (on Peace Brigades International), *Peace News*, November 27, 1981.
"International Peace Brigades and Nonviolent Army in India" (in Norwegian), *Var Verden* (Kongens gt. 94, 7000 Trondheim, Norway), Fall 1981.
"Peace Brigades," *Fellowship* (Box 271, Nyack, New York 10960), July-August 1982; *The Disarmament Catalog*, ed. Murray Polner, Pilgrim Press, New York, 1982; and *Shalom News*, December 1983.
"Peace Brigades" (short version, in Japanese), *Sarvodaya* (1-32, Kanda-Jinbocho, Chiyodaku, Tokyo-101, Japan), August 1982.
"Confessions of a Gandhian Spinner," *Textile Artist's Newsletter* (5533 College Avenue, Oakland, California 94618), Fall 1982.

Chapter 4
"Chipko: North India's Tree Huggers," *Coevolution Quarterly*, (now *Whole Earth Review*, Box 428, Sausalito, California 94966), Fall 1981; and *Hugging the Himalayas: The Chipko Experience*, ed. S.S. Kunwar, Dasholi Gram Swarajya Mandal, Gopeshwar (Chamoli), Uttar Pradesh, India, 1982.

Chapter 5
"The People's Court: Justice that Unites," *Communities* (126 Sun St., Stelle, Illinois 60919), Winter 1984–5.

Chapter 6
"Danagram Village: The Joy of Unity," *Communities*, April 1981.
"Sevamandir School: Back to Basics, Indian-Style," *The Unicorn* (400 Lake St., Ithaca, New York 14850), Fall 1981.

All photos by the author unless otherwise noted.

I must warn you against the impression that mine is the final word on nonviolence. All I claim is that every experiment of mine has deepened my faith in nonviolence as the greatest force at the disposal of mankind.

◄ Gandhi

I don't know which is the greater task: to decentralize a top-heavy civilization or to prevent an ancient civilization from becoming centralized and top-heavy. In both cases the core of the problem is to discover what constitutes a good civilization, then proclaim it to the people and help them to erect it.

◄ Gandhi

The impact of a man like Gandhi is not to be measured over two years or four years or twenty years. The ideas he has given us are imperishable.

◄ Vinoba Bhave

1 *Prologue: The Legacy*

I am not interested in freeing India merely from the English yoke. I am bent on freeing India from any yoke whatever.

◄ Gandhi

I can combine the greatest love with the greatest opposition to wrong.

◄ Gandhi

I do not believe in the doctrine of the greatest good of the greatest number. The only real, dignified, human doctrine is the greatest good of all.

◄ Gandhi

At midday on January 31, 1948, a modified military vehicle moved into the streets of New Delhi, carrying in an open coffin the body of Mohandas K. Gandhi, slain the day before by an assassin's bullet.

Colleagues and friends of the Mahatma—"Great Soul," as a nation proclaimed him—sat by the coffin on the platform of the vehicle as it was pulled by rope by 200 troops from India's new armed forces. Thousands of other troops and police marched ahead and behind. The procession inched its way through a mourning multitude, an estimated million people, while another million and a half followed behind.

1

Courtesy of the Gandhi Museum, New Delhi

There were frequent shouts of "Mahatma Gandhi ki jai!"—
"Victory to Mahatma Gandhi!"—the old liberation rallying cry;
at other times the crowd took up sacred chants. Armored cars,
police, and soldiers maintained order. Three military planes flew
overhead and dropped rose petals from the sky.

The procession traveled five and a half miles in almost as many
hours. It finally reached the banks of the river Jumna, where the
funeral pyre had been built and where a million more people
waited. Gandhi's body was laid on the piled logs, and, as the
crowd groaned, the pyre was set aflame.

Fourteen hours later the flames were spent, and Gandhi's ashes
were mingled with the ashes of the fire.

Probably no Indian has been mourned as widely and deeply as
Mahatma Gandhi. But the prominence of the military at the
funeral of this man of peace hovered over the event like an ironic
question mark.

Would India's new leaders continue on the path laid by
Gandhi?

Had they even understood it?

◄ ►

Gandhi had developed a means of political struggle powerful enough to rid India of British colonial rule, yet based on the highest moral principles. He called this form of nonviolent action *Satyagraha*, "Truth-force." (For a note on terms, see page viii.)

Gandhi experimented with several forms of Satyagraha:

◄ *Civil disobedience* was breaking specific laws, then accepting the legal penalties.

◄ *Noncooperation* was withdrawing support from an injustice by refusing to cooperate with it, no matter what the personal cost. This took such forms as strikes, economic boycotts, and tax refusals.

◄ *Fasting* was a form of Satyagraha often used by Gandhi as an individual action.

Though none of these forms was invented by Gandhi, he developed them further than anyone had before as a set of conscious political tools.

Gandhi not only developed their political effectiveness but also carried their nonviolence to an extreme. No physical *or* mental harm was to be inflicted on the opponent. Physical coercion *and* direct psychological coercion were ruled out. Even secrecy was renounced—the opponent was informed of all planned moves.

Courtesy of the Gandhi Centenary Committee

Then how did Satyagraha work?

Several principles seem to have operated. One important element of Satyagraha was willingly accepting suffering. For their actions, Gandhi's followers were beaten, went obligingly to jail, or had their property confiscated—all without lifting a hand to resist. This self-sacrifice was meant to arouse the opponent's conscience and finally bring about a change of heart.

In practice, its more telling effect may have been to arouse public opinion in favor of the sufferers, which brought strong pressure against the opponent.

The other important element was noncooperation. Gandhi pointed out that the power of a tyrant depended on people's willingness to obey. If people refused to obey—whatever the personal cost—the tyrant's power was ended. In practice, noncooperation made India increasingly hard for Britain to govern.

Satyagraha was idealistic but at the same time intensely practical. It was a source of power for a people that had neither weapons nor wealth. It gave the British no way to justify their violent repression. And, by ruling out the return of blows, it avoided generating a British will to fight harder—as often happens in violent struggle. In fact, Satyagraha allowed India and Britain to end their conflict not as bitter enemies but as friendly partners within the British Commonwealth.

Satyagraha had longer-term advantages as well.

Gandhi believed that the means of struggle a people used would shape the society that grew out of the struggle. Violent revolutions, he noted, almost always ended with the military victors setting up a repressive tyranny to uphold their gains. But a people practicing Satyagraha, he said, would gain the power, methods, and values needed to build a free, peaceful society.

As Gandhi put it, the means must be in accord with the end desired, because the means *become* the end. India, though it has been afflicted by widespread injustice, civil violence, and authoritarian trends, yet is one of the few Third World countries where democracy has survived continuously in any form.

Gandhi wrote, "All my actions have their source in my inalienable love of mankind." Love for the victim demanded struggle, even as love for the opponent ruled out doing harm. In fact, Gandhi believed love for the opponent likewise demanded struggle, because oppression corrupted the spirit of the oppressor. Satyagraha, then, was for the opponent's sake as well—not a way for one group to wrest what it wanted from another, but a way to remove injustice and restore social harmony, to the benefit of both sides.

When Satyagraha worked, both sides won.

This, more than any tactical innovation, was Gandhi's great and unique contribution: this spirit he infused into his campaigns, his integration of a high moral attitude with mass political struggle. It is for this that the world has declared him a pioneer of the human spirit.

◄ ►

Still, it was not political struggle that Gandhi considered his most important work. Even more important to him was what he called "constructive work"—efforts to transform Indian society.

Though Gandhi believed that British rule was greatly harming India, he did not believe that getting rid of the British would alone solve India's problems. And if they weren't solved, he said, India without the British would be as bad off as India with the British. Besides, in Gandhi's mind, strengthening Indian society was also the best way to combat the British—since it was only India's weaknesses that allowed Britain to rule.

So, alongside the political struggle for independence, Gandhi set thousands of Indians to work on a wide-ranging "constructive program." This program aimed to heal the divisions between Hindus and Muslims; to end the oppression of the Untouchables, outcasts from the Hindu social order; to combat backward social practices, such as child marriage and dowry; and to improve sanitary practices.

Above all, the program tried to inject new economic strength into India's villages. It sought to improve village agriculture and, even more, to revive neglected village crafts. Gandhi believed that the villagers' purchase of clothes and other goods made by urban factories—both British and Indian—was sucking the life-

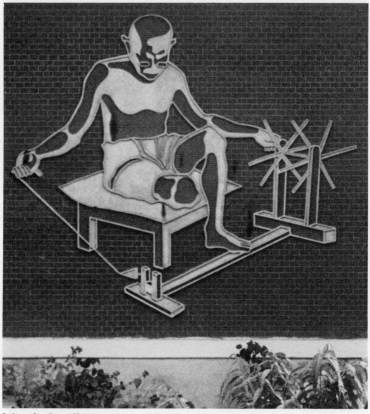

Mural, Gandhi Institute of Studies, Benares

blood of village economies and ensuring the villagers' own poverty and degradation.

Gandhi did not believe that a healthy society could ever be built on cities and factories.

An industrial economy, he said, stole work from humans and gave it to machines, while dehumanizing the workers retained to mind them. It split society into antagonistic classes of ownership and labor. It generated ever more powerful government to regulate and support it—government that more and more restricted individual freedom, whether that government was communist, socialist, or capitalist.

In league with the government it fostered, this industrial economy was then forced to exploit weaker countries just to maintain itself—as Britain was exploiting India. And, once its tentacles were firmly rooted in parts of the globe where it had no justifiable business, it led its government into international wars to protect its "economic interests"—while producing ever more deadly weapons for fighting those wars.

This type of economy and society were what native political leaders throughout the Third World wanted for their own countries, in their eagerness to imitate the rich nations of the West. But Gandhi demurred.

India could become strong and healthy, Gandhi insisted, only by revitalizing its villages, where over four-fifths of its people lived—a figure that still applies today. He envisioned a society of strong villages, each one politically autonomous and economically self-reliant. In fact, Gandhi may be this century's greatest proponent of decentralism—basing economic and political power at the local level. (E. F. Schumacher, the best-known decentralist thinker of recent years, called Gandhi "the most important economic teacher today," and drew from the writings of Gandhian economists such as Richard Gregg and J. C. Kumarappa.)

Only in villages, Gandhi believed, might be forged an alternative to the system of greed and violence ravaging the planet. Only there, where people were face to face, might they learn to hold each other in mutual bonds of fellowship and responsibility. And only in this way might a society be built devoted not to the welfare of a few, or even of a majority, but to the "welfare of all."

A society for the welfare of all. That was what Gandhi's constructive program aimed at. It was what his insatiable love of humankind demanded.

He would settle for nothing less.

◄ ►

Each of these parallel branches of Gandhi's work—political struggle and constructive work—was entrusted to a different group.

The independence struggle was the work of the Indian National Congress (commonly called "the Congress"), a nongovernment organization that came under Gandhi's leadership soon after his return from South Africa and that he then reorganized.

Constructive work was handled by a host of allied organizations, each one set up by Gandhi to oversee a particular part of his program. In his later years, Gandhi devoted himself more and more to these constructive work agencies, while the Congress grew more and more independent of him.

Of course, political and constructive efforts overlapped. Village constructive workers promoted the independence cause, and the Congress supported the constructive program.

But support of the constructive program by the Congress was generally halfhearted. Congress leaders saw constructive work as a way to win the allegiance of India's masses for the independence struggle; few were much interested in village development for its own sake. Being themselves mostly members of the urban, British-educated elite, they longed to see India grow into a strong industrial nation, like those in the West.

The differences between Gandhi and most of his political colleagues became even clearer as India's Independence Day, August 15, 1947, drew near.

The Indian National Congress was taking on leadership of the government—a position it would continue to hold as the dominant political party in the new democracy. Congress leaders who had willingly gone to prison for the cause of independence suddenly were seen assuming the regal style of the departing British. With apparent relish, they settled into the lavish edifices of New Delhi, taking their places at the head of the massive government bureaucracy.

In many ways, it was as if British rule were continuing, but with Indian names and faces at the top.

Now that these Congress leaders were safely in power, Gandhi was more and more often bypassed on important issues. After his assassination on January 30, 1948, his followers discovered they had little influence at all. It became clear that the politicians controlling the government had no interest in adopting Gandhian social and economic policies. The leaders were also content to use the country's armed forces in internal and international conflicts, discarding nonviolent action now that arms were at hand.

Of course, not all Congress leaders were so ready to discard Gandhi's principles. One notable exception was Jawaharlal Nehru, prime minister for the nation's first seventeen years. As he gained more independence in leadership, Nehru managed to set up a number of programs to help India's villages—though, in practice, these were usually thwarted or monopolized by the rural rich, actually leaving the poor worse off than before.

Yet even Nehru was far from committed to the whole of Gandhi's vision. While supporting village industries, he worked much harder to encourage the urban factories whose competition ruined the village enterprises. While striving in the cause of world peace, he began the military buildup that in time gave India the fourth largest armed force in the world.

What then had become of the Gandhian tradition in India? Had it quietly died away? What about the "army" of constructive workers Gandhi sent to the villages?

Were there still Indians who believed in his philosophy and methods, committed to finishing the work he began?

If so, what were they doing now?

◀ ▶

I was inspired to seek answers to these questions when, in late 1977 in San Francisco, I met a modern-day Gandhian named K. Krishnan Nair.

"The Indian revolution has two aspects," Nair told me. "The first phase we have achieved—that is, liberating our country from foreign domination. The second phase is the complete restructuring of our society.

"Until we complete this work, we'll not be sitting quiet."

Nair urged me to come to India to see for myself the current work of the Gandhians. Taking up this challenge, I traveled to India in October 1978, to spend the next five months visiting and living with Gandhians, learning about their projects, their ideas, their lives.

I found that the tradition begun by Gandhi is very much alive. In fact, it has grown much since Gandhi's time, with new faces, new issues, new ideas, new techniques, new failures, and new successes. Though in some ways it may have fallen back from the standard Gandhi set, in other ways it has gone beyond him.

I offer what I found, in the hope that others too may discover in it signposts along the road to a more just and peaceful society—a society for the welfare of all.

2 The Saint and the Socialist

All revolutions are spiritual at the source. All my activities have the sole purpose of achieving a union of hearts.
◄ Vinoba Bhave

Salvation will not come from the legislators. Salvation will not come from the military. If there is any salvation, it will come from the people.
◄ Jayaprakash Narayan

It would be hard to imagine two people less alike than the two who, next to Gandhi, have done most to mold the Gandhian movement of India today.

Vinoba Bhave (pronounced Bah-vay) was known as Gandhi's spiritual heir. He was considered a saint in the Hindu tradition, even by many of his critics.

Jayaprakash Narayan—commonly called JP—was considered Gandhi's political heir by many Gandhians. He was most like a Western intellectual in thought and style.

Vinoba was known for his serenity. JP was a man of stone-faced exterior but turbulent emotions.

Vinoba preferred solitude. JP thrived on action in the field.

But some characteristics were common to both: great compassion, selfless dedication, and relentless energy.

◄ ►

Vinoba Bhave, 1978

In 1916, at the age of twenty, Vinoba Bhave was in the holy city of Benares, studying Sanskrit scriptures and trying to come to a decision:

Should he go to the Himalaya mountains and become a religious hermit?

Or should he go to West Bengal and join the guerrillas fighting the British?

Then Vinoba came across a newspaper account of a speech by Gandhi, who had confronted an audience of British officials and Indian maharajas—condemning their ostentatious riches and calling for national liberation through nonviolent means. Vinoba was thrilled. Soon after, he joined Gandhi in his ashram near the western Indian city of Ahmedabad. (An *ashram* is a religious community—but for Gandhians, it is also a center for political and social action.)

As Vinoba later said, he found in Gandhi the peace of the Himalayas united with the revolutionary fervor of Bengal.

Vinoba spent five years with Gandhi in the Ahmedabad ashram, impressing the other ashramites with both his religious scholarship and his devotion to hard labor. Then Gandhi sent him to manage a succession of branch ashrams near the city of Wardha, in central India. Over time, Vinoba also led several nonviolent action campaigns under Gandhi's supervision and spent much time in jail.

Gandhi greatly admired Vinoba, commenting that Vinoba understood Gandhian thought better than he himself did. In 1940 he showed his regard by choosing Vinoba over Nehru to lead off a national protest campaign against British war policies.

After Gandhi's assassination on January 30, 1948, many of Gandhi's followers looked to Vinoba for direction.

A conference of Gandhian political leaders and constructive workers was held in March at Sevagram Ashram near Wardha, where Gandhi had moved in 1936. (The ashram Vinoba headed was in the village of Paunar, a few miles from Sevagram.) Vinoba told the gathering that, now that India had reached its goal of *Swaraj*—independence, or self-rule—the Gandhians' new goal should be a society dedicated to *Sarvodaya*, the "welfare of all."

The name stuck, and the movement of the Gandhians became known as the Sarvodaya Movement.

Not long after the conference, some of the constructive work agencies founded by Gandhi united to form Sarva Seva Sangh, the "Society for the Service of All." Though many other constructive workers stayed in separate organizations, or became part of government agencies, the Sangh became the core of the Sarvodaya Movement as the main organization working for broad social change along Gandhian lines. In time, membership reached 5,000 to 7,000 (though not all members were active), making the Sangh the largest nonpolitical, nonchurch private organization in India. And several times that number took part in Sangh campaigns at their peaks.

Many people saw Vinoba as *the* potential successor to Gandhi. But Vinoba didn't want to be a leader. He preferred to remain quietly in his ashram, where he and his close followers had begun an experiment in near-total self-sufficiency. He didn't even bother to attend the second annual Sarvodaya conference.

But the other Sarvodaya leaders weren't ready to let Vinoba fade into private life. In 1951, they threatened to cancel the third Sarvodaya conference if he again stayed away. So Vinoba agreed to come. He decided, though, to walk the entire distance—300 miles. Taking several colleagues with him, he spent a month visiting villages along the way, before arriving on time for the Sarvodaya conference in the central Indian state of Hyderabad (now part of Andhra Pradesh).

At the close of the conference, Vinoba announced he would continue his march. He had a mission to undertake in the nearby district of Telengana.

He couldn't have picked a more troubled spot.

◄ ►

Telengana was at that moment the scene of an armed insurrection. Communist students and some of the poorest villagers had united in a guerrilla army. This army had tried to break the land monopoly of the rich landlords by driving them out or killing them and distributing their land.

At the height of the revolt, the guerrillas had controlled an area of 3,000 villages. But the Indian army had been sent in and had begun its own campaign of terror. Now, many villages were occupied by government troops during the day and by Communists at night. Each side would kill villagers they suspected of supporting the other side. So most villagers lived in terror of both sides.

The government had clearly shown it would win, but the conflict wasn't nearly over by the time of the Sarvodaya conference. Vinoba hoped to find a solution both to the violence and to the injustice that had spawned it. So, refusing police escort, he and his small company set off.

On April 18, the third day of his walk, Vinoba stopped in the village of Pochampalli, which had been an important Communist stronghold. Setting himself up in the courtyard of a Muslim prayer compound, he was soon receiving visitors from all the factions in the village.

Among the visitors was a group of 40 families of landless Harijans. (*Harijan* was Gandhi's name for the Untouchables, the outcasts from Hindu society. Literally, it means "child of God.") The Harijans told Vinoba they had no choice but to support the Communists, because only the Communists would give them land. They asked, Would Vinoba ask the government instead to give them land?

Vinoba replied, "What use is government help until we can help ourselves?" But he himself wasn't satisfied by the answer. He was deeply perplexed.

Late that afternoon, by a lake next to the village, Vinoba held a prayer meeting, which drew thousands of villagers from the surrounding area. Near the beginning of the meeting, he presented the Harijans' problem to the assembly. Without really expecting a response, he said, "Brothers, is there anyone among you who can help these Harijan friends?"

A prominent farmer of the village stood up. "Sir, I am ready to give one hundred acres."

Vinoba could not believe his ears.

Here, in the midst of a civil war over land monopoly, was a farmer willing to part with 100 acres out of simple generosity.

And Vinoba was just as astounded when the Harijans declared that they needed only 80 acres and wouldn't accept more!

Vinoba suddenly saw a solution to the region's turmoil. In fact, the incident seemed to him a sign from God. At the close of the prayer meeting, he announced he would walk all through the region to collect gifts of land for the landless.

So began the movement called Bhoodan—"land gift." Over the next seven weeks, Vinoba asked for donations of land for the landless in 200 villages of Telengana. Calculating that one-fifth of India's farmland was needed to supply India's landless poor (he later revised this to one-sixth), he would tell the farmers and landlords in each village, "I am your fifth son. Give me my equal share of land." In each village—to his continued amazement—the donations poured in.

Who gave, and why?

At first most of the donors were farmers of moderate means, including some who themselves owned only an acre or two. To them, Vinoba was a holy man, a saint, the Mahatma's own son, who had come to give them God's message of kinship with their poorer neighbors. Vinoba's prayer meetings at times took on an almost evangelical fervor. As for Vinoba, he accepted gifts from even the poorest—though he sometimes returned these gifts to the donors—because his goal was as much to open hearts as to redistribute land.

But gradually the richer landowners also began to give. Of course, many of their gifts were inspired by fear of the Communists and hopes of buying off the poor—as the Communists were quick to proclaim.

But not all the motives of the rich landowners were economic. Many of the rich hoped to gain "spiritual merit" through their gifts; or at least to uphold their prestige. After all, if poor farmers were willing to give sizable portions of their land to Vinoba, could the rich be seen to do less? And perhaps a few of the rich were even truly touched by Vinoba's message.

In any case, as Vinoba's tour gained momentum, even the announced approach of the "god who gives away land" was enough to prepare the landlords to part with some of their acreage.

Soon Vinoba was collecting hundreds of acres a day. What's more, wherever Vinoba moved, he began to dispel the climate of tension and fear that had plagued the region. In places where people had been afraid to assemble, thousands gathered to hear him—including the Communists.

At the end of seven weeks, Vinoba had collected over 12,000 acres. After he left, Sarvodaya workers continuing to collect land in his name received another 100,000 acres!

◄ ►

Vinoba returned on foot to his Paunar ashram; but he had not left behind his interest in Bhoodan. After all, the problem of land monopoly wasn't restricted to Telengana. In fact, it was probably the greatest source of poverty throughout most of rural India. Bhoodan, Vinoba believed, might be the remedy.

What's more, he was beginning to think Bhoodan might be the lever he needed to start a "nonviolent revolution"—a complete transformation of Indian society by peaceful means.

The root of oppression, he reasoned, is greed. If people could be led to overcome their possessiveness, a climate would be created in which social division and exploitation could be eliminated. As he later put it, "We do not aim at doing mere acts of kindness, but at creating a Kingdom of Kindness."

So Vinoba continued his Bhoodan pleas on a walk to New Delhi, and then began a tour of the adjoining state of Uttar Pradesh. Soon he and other Sarvodaya parties were collecting 1,000 acres a day, then 2,000, then 3,000.

Halfway through the year-long campaign, with 170,000 acres collected in Bhoodan campaigns so far, Vinoba set Sarva Seva Sangh a target of 50 million acres nationwide—one-sixth of India's cultivable land—and himself vowed to continue marching until that goal was reached. As a first step, he insisted on 2½ million acres by the 1954 Sarvodaya conference, two years away.

Sarva Seva Sangh mobilized to meet the challenge. Bhoodan became a nationwide movement. Meanwhile, Vinoba himself— after leading the collecting of 300,000 acres in Uttar Pradesh—turned his steps east to the neighboring state of Bihar.

Bihar had special meaning for Vinoba: It was the homeland of the Buddha, and it was the poorest state in India. So Vinoba decided to make Bihar a test case: If the Gandhians could quickly obtain fully one-sixth of the farmland in Bihar—3 million acres— this would prove it could be done in India as a whole and would silence the skeptics.

But Bihar turned out to be more difficult than any area he had yet marched through.

Bihar's landlords were tough and hostile. In the first weeks, donations were only a few acres a day. Then, several months into the campaign, Vinoba was hit by a bad case of malaria. He at first refused to take medicine, though he was close to death. He finally relented and took a small dose of quinine, which caused an immediate improvement in his condition. But he required months to recover fully.

Vinoba's illness, though, turned out to be the turning point in the Bihar campaign. His plight touched the heart of the state. Hundreds of Sarvodaya workers and volunteers took to the Bhoodan trail to replace the ailing saint.

Before Vinoba had stirred from the village where he was re-covering, Bihar had donated over 400,000 acres.

Vinoba himself took up the march again as soon as he was able. With him always was a large company, made up of a few close assistants, a bevy of young, idealistic volunteers— teenagers and young adults, male and some female, mostly from towns or cities—plus maybe some regular Sarvodaya workers, a landlord, a politician, or an interested Westerner.

Each day Vinoba and his company would rise by 3:00 A.M. and hold a prayer meeting for themselves. Then they would walk ten or twelve miles to the next village, Vinoba leading at a pace that left the others struggling breathlessly behind. At the host village, they would be greeted by a brass band, a makeshift archway, garlands, formal welcomes by village leaders, and shouts of "Sant Vinoba, Sant Vinoba!" ("Saint Vinoba!")

After breakfast, the Bhoodan workers would fan out through the village, meeting the villagers, distributing literature, and taking pledges. Vinoba himself would be settled apart, meeting with visitors, reading newspapers, answering letters.

In late afternoon, there would be a prayer meeting, attended by hundreds or thousands of villagers from the area. After a period of reciting and chanting, Vinoba would speak to the crowd in his quiet, high-pitched voice. His talk would be completely improvised, full of rich images drawn from Hindu scripture or everyday life, exhorting the villagers to lives of love, kinship, sharing.

At the close of the meeting, more pledges would be taken. In the evening, Vinoba and his workers would meet to discuss accomplishments and plans.

There were no free weekends on this itinerary, no holidays, no days off. The man who led this relentless crusade was 57 years old, suffered from chronic dysentery, chronic malaria, and an intestinal ulcer, and restricted himself, because of his ulcer, to a diet of honey, milk, and yogurt.

Meanwhile, several hundred small teams of Sarvodaya workers and volunteers were likewise trekking from village to village, all over India, collecting land in Vinoba's name. As Vinoba's 1954 deadline approached, friends and detractors alike watched the movement in fascination. Even in the West, Vinoba's effort drew attention. In the United States, major articles on Vinoba had begun to appear—in the strait-laced *New York Times*, in the urbane *New Yorker*; Vinoba even appeared on the cover of *Time*.

By the eve of the April 18 Sarvodaya gathering—held near Bodh-Gaya, where Buddha is said to have reached Enlightenment—Vinoba's goal of 2½ million acres nationwide had been reached.

By the end of the four-day gathering, the nationwide total of donations had reached 3,200,000 acres.

◄ ►

But, even as the Sarvodaya workers were enjoying this triumph, serious problems were emerging.

Follow-up Sarvodaya teams were finding that much of the donated land wasn't fit for farming and that rich landowners often backed down on their commitments. Besides, the tremendous effort and sizable acreage collected in Bihar still hadn't come close to fulfilling the 3 million acre quota Vinoba had set for statewide donations in this test case.

As Vinoba continued his march through a succession of states, it became clear that the momentum leading up to the 1954 conference could not be sustained. Donations dwindled. After 1956, there were no more large gifts.

The movement seemed to have reached its saturation point at something over 4 million acres—less than a tenth of what Vinoba had said would solve India's land problem.

The Sarvodaya workers were disconcerted by this downturn in their prospects. Many hoped Vinoba would now turn to methods that more directly confronted the rich landowners—such as organizing the landless to nonviolently occupy the lands of the rich. But Vinoba opposed such methods, declaring them contrary to his objective of uniting hearts.

In any case, if Vinoba shared the misgivings of other Sarvodaya workers, he didn't show it. He was too busy shifting the movement to a new gear—a higher one.

Earlier, during the 1952 campaign in Uttar Pradesh, the village of Mangroth had become the first village to donate nearly *all* its land to Vinoba. It had in this way become the first *Gramdan*—"village-gift." Sarvodaya workers had been rushed to Mangroth to remake the village along Gandhian lines.

This example had grown on Vinoba. By 1955 he was asking for the donation of whole villages. By 1957 he was asking *only* for whole villages.

Sarva Seva Sangh again took Vinoba's lead, and Bhoodan gave way to Gramdan. By the end of that year, there were 3,500 Gramdan villages.

Gramdan was a far more radical program than Bhoodan. All village land was to be legally owned by the village as a whole, but parceled out for the use of individual families, according to need. Because the families could not themselves sell, rent, or mortgage the land, they could not be pressured off it during hard times—as normally happens when land reform programs bestow land title on the poor.

Village affairs were to be managed by a village council made up of all adult members of the village, making decisions by consensus—meaning the council could not adopt any decision until everyone accepted it. This would ensure cooperation and make it much harder for one person or group to benefit at the expense of others.

While Bhoodan had been meant to prepare people for a non-violent revolution, Vinoba saw Gramdan as the revolution itself.

Like Gandhi, Vinoba believed that the divisiveness of Indian society was a root cause of its degradation and stagnation. Before the villagers could begin to improve their lot, they needed to learn to work together. Gramdan, he felt, with its common land ownership and cooperative decision-making, could bring about the needed unity.

Once this had been achieved, the "people's power" it released would make anything possible.

Vinoba continued his walks through state after state. By 1960, about 5,000 villages had declared Gramdan; by 1964, about 7,000. But, in a country of 500,000 villages, this was a far cry from the sweeping nonviolent revolution the Gandhians sought—and the rate of collection was dropping. Besides that, most of the declared villages were small, single-caste, Harijan, or native tribal—not even typical Indian villages.

Gramdan seemed unable to regain the momentum Bhoodan had lost. In 1964, Vinoba left off his touring and returned to his Paunar ashram—for the first time in thirteen years! But, just a year later, in May 1965—in a determined effort to revive their movement—Vinoba and Sarva Seva Sangh eased the requirements for declaring a village Gramdan and launched a "storm campaign." The campaign was nationwide, but the focus was again on Bihar, where Vinoba took up residence to guide the effort.

Just as Bhoodan had been given impetus by the Communist revolt in Telengana, the renewed Gramdan campaign gained force from an unexpected event: a severe famine afflicting Bihar from 1965 to 1967. Hunger made the villagers more willing to consider the Gandhians' ideas of village cooperation—especially when they saw the technical and financial aid made available to other Gramdan villages.

The campaign began to pick up steam; it seemed to have finally recaptured the old momentum. The workers in Bihar soon gathered enough declarations in several "blocks" to declare the state's first "block-dans." (A *block* is a government administrative unit of 75–90 villages.)

By the end of 1966, the first "district-dan" was announced. Soon after, the Sarvodaya leaders raised their goal to "Bihar-dan," with a target date of October 2, 1969, the centennial of Gandhi's birth.

By that date, almost all the districts of Bihar had been declared district-dans; and Bihar-dan was officially proclaimed. By 1970 the official figure for Gramdan villages over the whole nation had reached 160,000—almost one-third of all India's villages. The Gandhian nonviolent revolution seemed within reach!

But the mirage soon faded.

The Sarvodaya workers discovered that it was easier to get a declaration of Gramdan than to set it up in practice. Often they found that the villagers' eagerness had cooled; and, since the requirements for the Gramdan declaration had been eased, rich and powerful families had been left out of many initial agreements.

What's more, the requirements had frequently been eased even further than the leaders had intended: In the Gandhians' enthusiasm, they had often declared Gramdan in a village without collecting the required percentage of signatures.

Another problem was that many of the Sarvodaya workers—themselves drawn mainly from India's rural and urban elite—weren't prepared to settle permanently for work among the village poor. Even if they all had been, there simply weren't enough workers or other resources to cover more than a fraction of the villages that had declared Gramdan.

By early 1970, only a few thousand villages had transferred land title to a village council. In most of these, not much more was done. By 1971, Gramdan as a movement had collapsed under its own weight and was uttering its last gasps.

Meanwhile, in June 1970, at the age of 74, Vinoba returned to his Paunar ashram. After thirteen years of continual marching, and five more of presiding over the Bihar "storm campaign," Vinoba's touring days were done.

◄ ►

Two decades of strenuous effort had failed to bring about a Gandhian social revolution. Still, Bhoodan and Gramdan were far from failures.

Bhoodan, with all its problems, had managed to distribute about 1⅓ million acres—far more than had been managed by the land reform programs of India's government.

As for Gramdan, there were at least 50 "pockets" where workers had settled in for long-term development efforts. Most of these consisted of native tribal, Harijan, or single-caste villages, which did not have the great problems of social division found in typical Indian villages. Still, the Gandhians' work there helped to benefit groups at the low end of the Indian social scale. The work in these villages also gave the Gandhians a chance to create models demonstrating their social vision and to work out ways of achieving it.

The Gandhians' expectations, though, had been much greater. With their hopes frustrated, and with Vinoba withdrawn, the stage was set for the emergence of a new leader.

That leader was Jayaprakash Narayan.

◄ ►

In 1921 Jayaprakash (JP) Narayan had answered Gandhi's call to the students of India by dropping out of his university to take part in the struggle for independence. But, the following year, JP decided to resume his studies and so boarded a cargo boat to the United States. He spent seven years at the University of California at Berkeley and several midwestern colleges. There he came in contact with a number of Communist students and professors. By the time JP returned to India in 1929, he was a confirmed Marxist.

On his return, JP joined the Indian National Congress and quickly distinguished himself in the independence struggle. In time he became the major spokesman for the socialist members of the Congress and became one of the chief critics of Gandhi's leadership. JP and the other socialists were frustrated by Gandhi's nonviolent methods, feeling that these were delaying independence and the remaking of Indian society.

Still, Gandhi and JP remained on cordial terms. Gandhi admired JP's sincerity and commitment, and he sometimes went out of his way to endorse a proposal of JP's or to recommend him for a position.

When World War II broke out, the British threw JP into prison for speaking against the war effort. Later, Gandhi was arrested on the eve of a nationwide campaign of civil disobedience. With Gandhi removed, mob violence swept the country, and armed insurrection erupted in some areas.

In the midst of this turmoil, JP and a few colleagues escaped from prison. JP went "underground," and spent the next year trying to organize armed resistance and sabotage. But the peak of the struggle had already passed, since the British had had no trouble putting down the scattered revolutionaries.

As JP later said, the British were even less threatened by violent tactics than he had thought they were by Gandhi's methods. Still, JP's exploits made him a legend among the people of India by the time he was recaptured and returned to prison.

JP was released several years later, as Britain finally prepared to grant India independence. The socialists in the Indian National Congress now broke away from the Congress to form the independent Socialist party, and installed JP as director.

JP, though, had entered a period of self-questioning—a questioning that had its origin in his disillusionment over the direction Communism had taken in the Soviet Union. Now the questioning intensified as JP watched in horror the Hindu–Muslim violence surrounding Independence, culminating in the assassination of Gandhi. He wondered whether Marxism, with its call for violent class struggle and a "dictatorship of the proletariat," could ever bring about the kind of society he yearned for. It seemed Gandhi had been right after all to insist that good ends required good means.

In 1951, Vinoba began his Bhoodan march. JP was impressed

Jayaprakash Narayan

Photo by R. K. Sharma

by this method of changing society that united people instead of dividing them.

The following year, he took part in the Bihar campaign, heading his own Bhoodan team. He also visited Mangroth, the village that had become the first Gramdan. There he became excited by an approach to revolution that helped villagers take charge of their own lives and not rely on a strong government to impose change from above.

Meanwhile, JP continued as director of the Socialist party, which was slowly moving toward a platform of democratic socialism. At one point, Nehru offered JP a government position with power second only to his own. Few politicians could have resisted the offer; but JP turned it down when Nehru declined to commit the government to the socialists' program. Even so, many people in political circles believed JP was popular enough to succeed Nehru as prime minister.

But JP was losing interest in party politics. More and more he felt that the place of a revolutionary was not in the halls of New Delhi but in the villages.

In late 1953, he resigned as director of the Socialist party. Finally, at the 1954 Bihar Sarvodaya conference—the one marking fulfillment of Vinoba's 2½ million acre quota for donations nationwide—JP astounded the assembly by completely renouncing party politics and offering himself to Bhoodan as the first *jivandan*, "life-gift."

◄ ►

JP's abilities and hard work soon gave him a position in the Sarvodaya Movement second only to Vinoba's. But the tasks JP took on over the next decade and a half were usually ones Vinoba wasn't concerned with; so JP's activities tended to broaden the movement's focus.

He traveled widely and became Sarvodaya's main spokesman in India's cities and in the West. He often commented on national and international politics, and he led Sarva Seva Sangh to do likewise. Twice he helped mediate armed conflicts between the central government and regional separatist forces. A number of times he organized massive famine and flood relief operations. In 1971, JP alerted the world to Pakistan's campaign of genocide in Bangladesh (previously East Pakistan).

JP's different outlook and interests were often reflected in differences of opinion with Vinoba. As Bhoodan cooled and Gramdan initially failed to heat up, JP was among the many Sangh workers who favored organizing the landless to nonviolently occupy the lands of the rich. Many of the Gandhians were ready to follow JP on this matter; but it would have meant challenging Vinoba's leadership, which JP wasn't willing to do.

With the collapse of the Gramdan "storm campaign," though, JP determined to seek new approaches.

Among these was a strengthened attention to issues of national politics. Though JP was still convinced the revolution he sought had to be built from the grass roots, he was also certain it could succeed only within the framework of a functioning democracy.

India's democracy wasn't functioning.

One serious problem with the government was corruption, which had become epidemic since Independence. It was now almost impossible to deal with the government without greasing someone's palm; and huge amounts of public money were disappearing into private pockets. Elections were more and more marked by vote-buying, extortion of money for campaign funds, rigging, and violence. JP believed government corruption had created a climate of immorality that infected the entire society.

Another problem was the firm hold on power of the Indian National Congress. After leading India to independence, the Congress had converted itself into a conventional political party, which had dominated India's politics ever since. (The Indian National Congress, commonly called "the Congress," is not to be confused with India's legislature, Parliament.)

With a history of mass organization dating back to the early days of the independence struggle, the Congress's political machinery was far stronger and more extensive than that of any of the parties opposing it. On top of that, the opposition was split into many small parties, ensuring continued victories for the Congress in national elections, even though the party never received an absolute majority of votes.

India's democracy had become a virtual one-party rule; and the Congress's secure position enabled Congress politicians to safely ignore the needs and desires of India's masses.

These problems of India's democracy had troubled JP for some time. Now a new one had emerged that seemed to lend the others greater urgency: the career of Indira Gandhi.

Indira Gandhi—no relation to the Mahatma, the name Gandhi having come to her by marriage—was the daughter of Nehru. She had been made prime minister by Congress party leaders in 1966, two years after her father's death. Since then, she had been greatly extending her personal political power, both within the Congress party and within the Indian government, at the expense of the legislature and the judiciary. She was also arranging changes in the Indian Constitution to weaken the guaranteed rights of individuals.

Mrs. Gandhi claimed that these measures were necessary to push through reforms for the benefit of India's masses—a claim that most Indians seemed to accept. But JP and other critics suspected this was simply a mask for personal ambition.

As JP turned his attention more to national politics, he began to speak out increasingly against Mrs. Gandhi's actions, and on the other issues that concerned him. With his longstanding reputation of selfless service, he was soon among the most formidable of the government's critics.

Then, unexpectedly, JP got a chance to move from words to action.

On March 15, 1974, university students in Bihar launched a movement against the Congress-led state administration, demanding that it end corruption, reduce unemployment, lower prices, and change the education system. The first day of statewide demonstrations was marked by police gunfire, which killed seven students. On March 18, the protesters' blockade of the state legislature in the capital city of Patna ended in a battle between police and students, with more police shooting and baton charges.

The movement's student leaders were unnerved by the violence. That evening they visited JP in his Patna home and asked him to organize the movement along nonviolent lines.

JP was at this time 70 years old, suffering from kidney and other physical problems, and about to undergo surgery. But he could hardly have refused. Leadership of the movement would give him a rich opportunity to mold the students' activism into a positive force. At the same time, it would provide a way to reclaim for the Gandhians their heritage of mass struggle.

So the alliance was struck between a group of college students and an aged Sarvodaya leader—an alliance that would create India's most powerful protest movement since the time of Gandhi.

◄ ►

JP quickly assembled a team of Sarvodaya workers to help him lead the movement and enlisted aid from many more Gandhians around the state. The Gandhians then guided the movement through a series of actions.

On April 8, a silent procession was held in Patna to protest the police killings. Yet, four days later, in another part of the state, police fired on demonstrators without reasonable provocation, killing eight more people.

Shortly after, the state's chief minister (the rough equivalent of a governor in the United States) shook up his cabinet in an attempt to placate the protesters. But the change was more show than substance, and JP labeled it a "cruel joke." JP now allowed the students to add two more demands to their list: the resignation of the chief minister and the dissolving of the state legislature to bring on new elections.

A mass rally was organized for June 5 in Patna. On that day, the government canceled buses and trains coming to Patna from around the state and stopped vehicles on the road. Still, an estimated half million people attended the rally. Addressing the crowd, JP called on the people of Bihar to paralyze the government, close the universities, and organize local action committees around the state. JP told the crowd that this movement was the first step toward a "Total Revolution"—a complete remaking of Indian society along Gandhian lines.

From this time on, "Total Revolution" became the rallying cry of the Bihar Movement, and of much of the Sarvodaya Movement as well.

Over the next month, protesters set up a daily "blockade" of the Patna legislature. When a legislator insisted on crossing their picket line, the protesters would lie down, forcing the legislator to walk over their bodies. Three thousand protesters were arrested there during the month. Meanwhile, in cities and towns around the state, government work was mostly halted by similar blockades of government offices and courts. In mid-July, university students observed an almost total boycott of classes in the first week of school.

The Bihar protesters for the most part stuck strictly to non-violence, even when provoked; but the few scattered incidents of protester violence were used by the government to justify its own massive use of force. By August, 40,000 national troops were stationed in the state, and Bihar was like an armed camp. Yet even this military presence failed to stifle the campaign.

In early October, a three-day general strike halted almost all regular activity throughout the state. JP claimed the strike as proof that 90 percent of the people of Bihar supported his movement.

Another mass rally was called for November 4 in Patna, to be followed that same day by a blockade of the Secretariat (the state administrative building) and the homes of government officials.

Preparing for the day of the rally, the government placed 60,000 troops and police on alert around the state. In bus and railway stations, people who might be traveling to Patna were stopped, and many were arrested. On the day of the rally, all trains and buses to Patna were canceled.

In Patna itself, government forces maintained barricades and cordons throughout the city. Checkposts had been set up at all the city's normal entrances, while planes patrolled overhead to spot people coming in by other routes.

Even so, about 50,000 people—mostly young men—entered Patna for the rally.

On the morning of November 4, at the exact time scheduled

Photo by R. K. Sharma

JP and protesters teargassed by police, November 4, 1974, Patna.

for the rally, JP boarded a jeep at his Patna home and was driven toward the rally site. While taking a roundabout way to avoid confronting the police, the jeep came upon a crowd of young protesters rushing in the opposite direction. The young people had tried to reach the rally site and had been beaten back by police. Now they walked alongside JP's jeep, gathering more of their number as they went.

With the young people around his jeep, JP continued past a number of barricades, in defiance of orders and warnings from the armed troops maintaining them. By the time JP neared the rally site, he was leading an estimated 20,000 people.

The rally site was a large public meeting ground, with barriers now erected across every entrance. As JP's jeep approached, the police shot tear gas at those nearest JP. JP stepped down from the jeep and rebuked the police for attacking peaceful protesters.

Then, before the police realized what he was doing, he climbed over a barricade into the meeting ground.

Thousands of young people came pouring into the meeting ground from all directions, shouting slogans. The police attacked with tear gas and batons.

JP, badly affected by the tear gas, rested a while; then he climbed back over the barricade and began his march toward the Secretariat. The crowd soon made its way to him and followed behind.

JP and his followers continued their march past police barricades. Again and again, the police attacked the crowd behind JP with batons and tear gas. Each time, the crowd dispersed, then gathered again behind JP farther down the road. At one point the crowd grew to an estimated 40,000.

Finally, a contingent of national security police moved in for a concerted attack. Four state police had been assigned to protect JP himself from harm, but these too were beaten up. JP was hit by a baton blow and sank to the ground. At once he was surrounded by a wall of people trying to protect him from further harm. Some state police tried with their own batons to intercept further blows to JP. One of JP's defenders had his arm broken; another had his skull cracked. Even so, JP was hit twice more.

But JP soon rose and continued on his way.

He finally reached the home of the state's finance minister, where a crowd of young people once more gathered around him. The police began arresting several hundred of them and loading them onto buses. Then JP boarded one of the buses and demanded to be arrested, on the grounds that his crimes were the same as the young people's.

The police were confounded. They were apparently under orders not to arrest JP. After a while, they drove the bus to a spot near JP's home, hoping he would then leave the bus. But JP refused to get out.

Finally, late that night, he left the bus to visit 3,000 young people the police were keeping in the open without blankets or food.

◄ ►

Despite the showing of the November 4 rally and earlier actions, and despite a near paralysis of the state government, the state refused to bow to the movement's demands. JP had gradually come to realize it wasn't free to do so. It was Indira Gandhi in New Delhi who was calling the shots for the Congress politicians heading Bihar's administration.

Following the November 4 action, then, JP shifted the strategy of the Bihar Movement. Mass actions were dropped in favor of organizing Bihar's voters, so that the Congress party would be swept from power in the state at the following year's election. Meanwhile, JP began touring other states in an attempt to spread the movement.

He was setting his sights much higher now. Mrs. Gandhi and the national Congress party had shown themselves as the real opponents in the struggle, and JP was determined they should bow to the people's will—or be swept aside.

Helped now by a national coalition of opposition political parties, as well as by local Gandhian workers, the "JP Movement" began to spread over much of the country. In towns and cities across India, JP drew crowds unmatched since the time of Gandhi. On March 6, he led perhaps a quarter million marchers through the streets of New Delhi, to present a list of demands to government leaders at Parliament.

Jayaprakash Narayan, the incorruptible nationalist leader, who had never sought office for himself, who had committed himself selflessly to uplifting the common people of India—he seemed to many to have inherited Gandhi's mantle as the conscience of the nation. His supporters called him Loknayak, the "People's Leader." Even many Congress party politicians sympathized with him.

Some of his supporters suggested that he form a party and make a bid for the prime minister's office. JP wasn't interested.

Even so, it was becoming clear that India's politics did not have room for both JP and Mrs. Gandhi.

In June of that year (1975), two political reverses for Indira Gandhi suddenly made it look as if her removal was at hand.

A state election in Gujarat was won by an opposition party coalition supported by JP, even though Mrs. Gandhi had personally campaigned there for the Congress. On the same day these results were announced, the Uttar Pradesh High Court convicted Mrs. Gandhi of election malpractice. The conviction was on a minor charge; but, if upheld by India's Supreme Court, it would force her to leave office within six months and bar her from any public office for six years.

Opposition politicians and the press immediately called on Mrs. Gandhi to step down until her Supreme Court appeal was heard. At a mass rally in New Delhi on the evening of June 25, JP repeated this demand as he announced a new nationwide action campaign.

Demonstrations, he said, would be held in all state capitals, in local government centers, and daily in New Delhi itself. He called on all Indians to stop cooperating with the government and asked police officers and soldiers not to obey any orders violating India's Constitution.

After the rally, JP retired for the night to a nearby Gandhian headquarters.

A few hours later he was awakened by police.

A state of national emergency had been declared, they informed him. He was under arrest.

◄ ►

Hundreds of other movement leaders were arrested the same night, and thousands more over the next several weeks. Included were several hundred Sarvodaya workers who had been active in JP's movement, as well as opposition party leaders, and even critics of Mrs. Gandhi within the Congress party itself. (The number of political prisoners arrested during the Emergency eventually topped 100,000, rivaling arrests made by the British following Gandhi's Salt March.) All were imprisoned without trial or formal charges, under the emergency provisions of

India's Constitution. At the same time, strict censorship was clamped on the media.

Over the first few days of the Emergency, thousands of general strikes, rallies, and silent processions sprang up in cities and towns around the country, expressing outrage at Mrs. Gandhi's action. But her surprise counterattack had left her opponents leaderless, unorganized, and isolated from each other. Despite continuing scattered acts of peaceful resistance—mostly organized by opposition political leaders in hiding—the uproar of protest soon died away, replaced by a climate of fear. Meanwhile, Mrs. Gandhi and her colleagues moved quickly to strengthen their position by passing a series of laws and constitutional amendments increasing their powers, at the same time launching an ambitious program of social and government reform.

Of course, not all Indians were opposed to the Emergency. Many accepted Mrs. Gandhi's view of the JP Movement as a ploy by opposition parties to circumvent the democratic process, remove Mrs. Gandhi by mob pressure, and take power for themselves. Many Indians, distressed over the growing chaos of India's economy and politics, were only too happy to have Mrs. Gandhi take a strong hand.

A similar viewpoint could be found even within the Sarvodaya Movement. Though most of the Sangh workers had given JP active or moral support, Vinoba and some of his closest followers had opposed JP's movement from the start.

Vinoba had criticized it for having an antagonistic spirit; for diverting the energies of Sangh workers from their more important work in the villages; and for threatening the Sangh's broad, nonpartisan base of support by drawing the Sangh into the rivalries of party politics. Vinoba had also said the movement would accomplish nothing.

The disagreement had come to a head a few months before the Emergency. In March 1975, Vinoba and his close followers—about a seventh of Sarva Seva Sangh's membership—had formally broken with the Sangh.

Now Vinoba's followers—though not Vinoba himself—said that the declaration of Emergency had been justified by JP's irresponsible actions.

JP himself, placed in isolation by the government, spent the first few months of the Emergency in anguish at the thought that his attempt to save India's democracy had led to its downfall.

In September he started having severe cramps. On November 14 he was released just hours before he was expected to die. JP lived—but doctors discovered that his kidneys had almost stopped working. From then on, his life would depend on regular dialysis, a blood purification treatment using sophisticated machinery.

JP was now technically an invalid, but he refused to let that stop him. After resting for several months, he was again touring the country, trying to raise opposition to Mrs. Gandhi.

Then, on January 18, 1977—nineteen months after the declaration of emergency—Mrs. Gandhi astonished the nation and the world by "relaxing" the Emergency and calling for elections. Most political prisoners were released, and press censorship was lifted. But Mrs. Gandhi wasn't making it easy for the opposition parties. She was giving them only two months before the elections to rebuild their strength and organize a viable campaign. There seemed little chance they could do it. Besides, the opposition remained fragmented into many small parties. This would ensure a Congress party victory, as it always had.

But the election campaign held some surprises in store.

Spurred by JP, the opposition parties that had supported him announced their merger into a Janata ("People's") party. Later, the new party was augmented by a major group defection from the Congress party itself.

Following the launching of the party, JP threw himself into a campaign to raise support for it. Three days in the week, JP was hooked to a machine that moved the blood out of his body, purified it, and pumped it back in. Every other day, he was traveling the country, canvassing and speaking to mass rallies.

His basic message was simple: You will vote for either democracy or dictatorship—and it may be your last chance.

That March, the Indian voters appeared to have heard JP's message. In its first national defeat since Independence, the Congress party was overwhelmingly swept out of power, while the Janata party was swept in.

On March 22, 1977, Indira Gandhi revoked the Emergency and resigned as prime minister of India.

In JP's eyes, though, the struggle was far from over. He hoped that now, under a sympathetic government, his Total Revolution might yet be made a reality. Even as the Janata leaders were assuming office, JP was calling for a national campaign to set up local "people's committees" that would watchdog the government and fight injustice.

◄ ►

By the time of my India visit—late 1978—JP's hopes had proved false.

The momentum of his movement had been lost and could not be regained. Most of JP's supporters had been interested only in changing the leaders who governed them, not in taking into their own hands the remaking of their society.

As for the Janata party, though its leaders had promised to govern by Gandhian principles, their policies had turned out to be little different from those of their Congress party predecessors. What's more, they were helping Mrs. Gandhi to a political comeback, by their infighting and by their legal persecution of Mrs. Gandhi, which was giving her a martyr's image.

At the end of 1978, Mrs. Gandhi regained a seat in Parliament. In the summer of 1979, she managed to split the Janata party by playing on the ambitions of its leaders, bringing about the collapse of the Janata government. The subsequent elections in January 1980 returned to her the office of prime minister. (Following her return to power, local and national harassment of the Gandhians confirmed Vinoba's final fear about JP's movement.)

JP, too sick now to have much influence, could do little but watch events unfold. On October 8, 1979, he passed away—a death marked by funeral crowds of a size reportedly unmatched since the passing of Nehru.

Vinoba followed on November 15, 1982. In his dying, as in his living, he was deliberate, instructive, and, in a way, lighthearted. After suffering a heart attack in early November, Vinoba decided to "leave his body before his body left him." He therefore simply stopped eating until his body released him.

Indira Gandhi was assassinated on October 31, 1984, by Sikh separatists. In her final years, she seemed determined to establish a family dynasty; and she succeeded—at least for the time being—through her son, Rajiv Gandhi, who was made prime minister following her death. Fortunately, Rajiv has proved to be a distinct improvement over his mother—and most other Indian politicians—in his manner of governing. Reaction from the Gandhians, though, has been mixed.

The Gandhians have slowly recovered from the blows of the Emergency, from the split between Vinoba's supporters and JP's, and from the deaths of their two major figures. But the Gandhian leadership remains largely divided between adherents of Vinoba and those of JP.

Vinoba's branch of the movement, now centered in Vinoba's Paunar ashram, promotes several programs sponsored by Vinoba since the demise of the Gramdan storm campaign.

For instance, Women's Power Awakening, a movement led by Vinoba's women disciples, is a Gandhian version of women's liberation. Like Gandhi, Vinoba believed that women were specially suited to a loving nonviolence, and so had more to contribute than men to building a nonviolent society. The broad goal of Women's Power Awakening is to awaken women to their special abilities—which in part requires freeing them from present oppression.

As of 1986, the main effort of Vinoba's followers is a campaign against "cow slaughter," an issue long important to Gandhians for its relation not only to nonviolence but also to India's pattern of self-sufficient agriculture. Useful plow and dairy animals are being butchered for meat—not only to feed the meat-eating minority in India but also for export.

On the side of the Gandhian movement formerly led by JP, the leadership of Sarva Seva Sangh is now shared by a few figures.

Following the Janata party's election victory, the Sangh undertook to organize JP's "people's committees" to conduct local struggles against injustice and watchdog the government; but this effort failed to arouse much public interest. The official organizing body, the National People's Committee, has remained an adjunct of the Sangh, as the major medium for the Sangh's resumed criticism of the Congress government.

More importantly, the Sangh is committed to strengthening existing Sarvodaya "pockets"—now about 150 of them nationwide.

The Sangh now calls these pockets "centers for Total Revolution," and the name change is significant. In a shift of approach begun in some places just after the demise of the Gramdan storm campaign, workers in a number of locations are organizing villagers for nonviolent struggle against injustice. For example, in Bihar and Tamilnadu states, villagers are being led to occupy land legally due them but in the hands of rich landlords and religious orders.

◄ ►

With the passing of Vinoba and JP, it is unlikely that the Sarvodaya Movement will again be a major force on a national level. But it may still provide guidance for an emerging generation of popular leaders grown increasingly willing to look back to Gandhi for inspiration.

Meanwhile, the Gandhians are a vital force in the many communities in which they have settled for long-term efforts. It is in these enclaves of Gandhian activity that the main strength of the Sarvodaya Movement is found today.

3 Soldier of Peace

Fearlessness is indispensable for the growth of the other noble qualities. How can one seek Truth, or cherish Love, without fearlessness?

◄ Gandhi

We are constantly being astonished at the amazing discoveries in the field of violence. But I maintain that far more undreamt of and seemingly impossible discoveries will be made in the field of nonviolence.

◄ Gandhi

It happened in a dormitory room at Sarva Seva Sangh's national headquarters in Benares, at a meeting to organize relief for flood victims in Bihar state.

In came Narayan Desai—head of the National People's Committee, director of training for Sarva Seva Sangh, right-hand man to Jayaprakash Narayan during the first months of the Bihar Movement, and longtime leader of Shanti Sena, the Gandhians' "Peace Army "—one of the top Gandhians. He was carrying a wooden box, about the size of a large telephone directory.

When he had settled himself cross-legged on a cot, he opened the box by a hinge at one end and began rearranging the contents. Soon, with one hand, he was turning a wheel inside the box. As the mechanism gave off a soft buzz, he drew out, with the other hand, a fine white line of cotton yarn. When his arm had stretched to its limit, he wound the yarn back onto a spinning metal needle and began again. He kept this up throughout

Narayan Desai

the meeting, gradually building a cone of white along the length of the needle.

The box was a *charkha*—a spinning wheel.

It was no accident or oddity that a major Gandhian was spinning cotton yarn during a serious meeting. In fact, it would have been stranger if Narayan had somehow in his life evaded the activity. After all, he was the son of Gandhi's chief secretary, Mahadev Desai, and had grown up in Gandhi's ashrams.

No program had been dearer to Gandhi than his effort to promote this modest skill.

Gandhi's concern for hand-spinning has often been misunderstood and scoffed at, but it was for the most part reasonable.

The British colonialists had suppressed India's textiles production—the country's single most important occupation after farming. They exported India's raw cotton, made it into cloth in British mills, and returned much of it for sale in India. This arrangement stole work from India's own hand-spinners and set up a steady flow of wealth out of India into the pockets of British mill owners. Gandhi believed this was the greatest cause of India's poverty. (Another cause, though—concentration of land holdings in the hands of rich Indians—was probably even more important, as Gandhi's successors eventually concluded.)

Gandhi insisted that India could never overcome its poverty or gain real independence until it revived its textile crafts. *Khadi*—homespun cloth—became the cornerstone of his constructive program, and the spinning wheel became his symbol of a nonviolent society.

To promote khadi, the Gandhians searched out traditional tools and techniques and improved them, but in ways that enabled them still to fit in with village life and resources. Narayan's charkha was an invention by Gandhi himself, using a double-wheel design to increase speed and control, while it reduced size. It represented probably the first conscious use of the principle of "intermediate technology."

Another way Gandhi tried to promote hand-spinning was to prescribe it as a national sacrament. He asked everyone in the country to spin at least a half hour a day. His closest followers spun much more than that, and Gandhi himself seldom went anywhere without a charkha or some other spinning tool.

Gandhi's khadi program actually had several faces. It began mainly as a relief program for poor villagers, a program that during Gandhi's lifetime would employ as many as half a million people (mostly women) at a time. In the years around 1930, khadi also was the basis of a national boycott of foreign cloth that forced many British mills to shut down.

As time went on, though, Gandhi began urging hand-spinning mainly as a way for India's villagers to move toward economic self-reliance. By reviving this and other village crafts, Gandhi hoped to stop the flow of money and jobs out of the villages—not only toward Britain but also toward the industrializing towns and cities of India itself. As Gandhi saw, this flow was slowly draining the lifeblood of the villages.

But this economic principle proved too abstract for the villagers; and besides, in the short run, hand-spinning for family use simply didn't pay. Under the new market conditions, by the time a family bought cotton, spun it, and paid to have it woven, it could have bought factory cloth at about the same price and saved the tremendous effort of spinning.

So the idea of khadi for self-reliance never caught on.

Khadi survives today mainly in the form of a relief employment program, overseen and subsidized by the government. In this program, the Gandhian spinning wheel has been replaced by a hand-cranked spinning machine of four or more spindles—which in turn is being replaced by foot-pedaled machines of six or twelve spindles.

These developments have greatly increased the spinners' rate of production and have for the first time made it possible for spinners to be paid a decent wage—but at the cost of much drudgery, as this delicate handcraft has descended to the level of mindless machine-cranking. Perhaps little better could be done, though, as things stand.

Meanwhile, some Gandhians still spin for the use of family and friends, both as a sacrament and as a witness for a village-based economy. As for Narayan—once the "fastest in India," as he told me—he had been spinning for 49 years, since the age of four. Nowadays his daily spinning was for him a soothing agent and an anchor.

"It is almost like a meditation," he said.

Few things could be more valuable than that, in a life as harrowing as Narayan's.

◄ ►

"The time was during World War II, when Japan was advancing on India. I was lying in my room one night, and my parents thought I was asleep. But I was just pretending to sleep, because, like all children in the world, I wanted to listen to my parents. So they were talking about me—which made me even more interested.

"The topic was this: That afternoon, Gandhi had said that if he had an army of nonviolent soldiers, he would like to defend the country nonviolently, by standing before the advancing Japanese troops. And so these two members of Gandhi's ashram were trying to decide which of them should join this army. Since they had a young, adolescent child, namely Narayan, they were thinking that one of them should stay behind. That way, at least one parent would survive.

"My mother was saying, 'He is nearly grown now, and you can probably look after him better. Let *me* join.'

"But my father was saying, 'Even if I remain behind, I might not have time to look after him. So *I* should join.'

"That was the kind of tussle going on. But in the end, they decided they would both join. They would leave Narayan in the hands of God.

"That was the first time I heard of Shanti Sena."

In his talk on the Gandhians' "Peace Army," Narayan Desai related that—though Gandhi called for a peace army for national defense in 1942 (a plan never tried, since the Japanese did not invade)—the idea of Shanti Sena was usually linked to combatting riots.

"Gandhi first used the term *Shanti Sena* in 1922, during the first large-scale riots between Hindus and Muslims in the years after his entry into the Indian political arena. My father organized some local units of Shanti Sena during riots in 1941. But it was only in 1947, the year of our Independence, that Gandhi considered organizing a nationwide Shanti Sena. This was a response to the rioting that at that time covered almost the entire north of what had been undivided India." In that holocaust, a half million people were slaughtered, and ten million driven from their homes, as united India was severed into India and Pakistan.

"Gandhi had invited a few hundred colleagues to come to his Sevagram Ashram and discuss organizing Shanti Sena. The conference was set for February 1948. Two days before the end of January, Gandhi was assassinated. So the conference was never held.

"But the idea was revived in 1957, in another emergency situation. Vinoba had just walked through an area of southern India where he had collected many Gramdan villages. In the adjacent district, there were riots between Hindus and Muslims. Vinoba said, 'If we have communal riots in the Gramdan villages, then our whole effort of creating united village communities will fail.' This is what led Vinoba to take up the idea of Shanti Sena."

Vinoba's first attempts to set up Shanti Sena proved unsuccessful. In 1962, chairmanship was passed to Jayaprakash Narayan, and Narayan Desai became Shanti Sena's director, a position he held until 1978. Under the leadership of these two, membership reached a high of about 6,000, in the mid-1960s.

Most of these Shanti Sainiks—"peace soldiers"—were regular Sarvodaya workers from rural areas, who might take part in Shanti Sena actions when rioting broke out in nearby towns or cities. In 1986, the unofficial makeup of Shanti Sena is much the same—though, as a formal organization, Shanti Sena has yet to recover fully from the Emergency and the split in the Sarvodaya Movement.

Riots are a major plague of India. Riots may stem from differences in religion, language and culture, or political party; or they may be by protesting university students. The worst rioting, though, is between Hindus and Muslims, with the majority Hindus usually the aggressors.

Some of these riots are more like miniature civil wars.

"Arson and looting are common," Narayan said. "Most of the direct violence against people is rock-throwing. But the knife is also used a great deal. In one riot, more than a thousand people were killed this way. Pistols and bombs are not used very much, but only because we don't have many firearms in India. Perhaps if we had them, there would be even greater violence."

The first step for a group of Shanti Sainiks that has decided to intervene in a riot is a public announcement, through newspapers and possibly radio. This publicity helps ease the approach to various figures in the conflict, and also serves to invite Shanti Sainiks of other areas to join up with that group. The announcement also might include a brief, impartial statement on the issues, establishing the Sainiks' nonpartisan stance.

The Sainiks arrive in the city over the course of the next few days, coming by train. There might eventually be 30 or more Sainiks working in a city. As they gather, they divide into teams.

"The first team meets with leaders of the communities involved in the riot, as well as with other important figures. We present ourselves not as saviors but as people eager to assist them in their difficulty. We gather information from them and try to understand their minds. And we try to find the forces of peace on both sides. Often there are people who favor peace but do not know how to work for it.

"In one city, we met with the top police officer and requested him not to fire on the rioting crowds, which so far he had avoided doing. When the police resort to firing, this means that several people die.

"He said, 'You are the first group asking me not to resort to firing. But there is a lot of political pressure on me to do it. What can I do?'

"So we met with this important political leader who was pressuring him. We knew that this political leader loved the city, so we asked him, 'Do you want the image of this city stained by blood?'

"He had no reply. Then we offered an alternative: 'You already have a curfew order in certain areas. Why not introduce it throughout the city?'

"So he immediately phoned the police officer and said, 'Instead of firing on the crowds, let's have a curfew order.'

"That officer was very happy to hear it."

Sometimes the Sainiks persuade leaders of opposing communities to call publicly for an end to violence, or to meet with leaders of the other side to begin talks.

"We usually try to organize some of these leaders into a peace committee. If the fighting is between Hindus and Muslims, we ask the Hindu community to suggest Muslim names for the committee, and vice versa.

"This is often very difficult, because tensions are very high. But once, say, the Hindus find out that the Muslims have given some Hindu names, they start thinking, yes, maybe they also can find names of some Muslims. And that creates joint committees in situations where people would not imagine that Hindus and Muslims could work together."

Most of the Sainik teams patrol areas of likely violence. The patrols talk to people on the street, and even in their houses, to find out what is on their minds and to convince them of the need to restore peace. Their presence alone also discourages violence.

"In one place in the city of Baroda we came upon a huge pile of rocks. So we asked the people standing there what the rocks were for. They said, 'These are country-made bombs. We'll use them at the proper time'—meaning, when there was a lone policeman or sentry going around. So we said, 'We guess you'll have to use them on us instead.'

"Some of them were angry, but others thought about it, and said they would find a better place. They thought, this wasn't the right place because there was somebody watching. But there was 'somebody watching' all over the city." Though there weren't that many Sainiks in the city, only downtown areas were affected by the rioting, and the Sainik teams had stationed themselves at all the crucial spots. Other times, when their numbers are even fewer, teams move from spot to spot.

But sometimes the Sainiks cannot prevent violence through their presence or persuasion. In those cases, they block it with their bodies. Dressed in their distinctive uniforms of white khadi with saffron scarves, they rush among the rioters, exhorting them or shouting peace slogans.

"Very often we have faced rock-throwing from both sides—or

rock-throwing from one side and batons or tear gas shells from the other, if government forces were involved. Fortunately, no stabbings.

"Women participate in this direct intervention as well as men. In fact, they are more successful at it, because they are less likely to be attacked."

One team of Sainiks might have the special job of fighting rumors.

"Rumors are one of the chief causes of violence in riots. When people are afraid, they tend to believe almost anything they hear. Figures get exaggerated. A story could grow until people think a thousand people have been killed on the other side of town, when nobody has been killed at all.

"Sometimes too there is a deliberate effort to create rumors." The Sainiks had known groups of troublemakers to travel around a city for hours spreading false stories.

Such stories were sometimes spread by the media as well. "In the city of Ahmedabad, one of the most widely read newspapers had a banner headline saying, 'Woman's breasts cut off in such and such location.' The newspaper did not say that a Muslim had cut off the breasts of a Hindu woman, but it as much as said that, because everyone knew that the mentioned area was Hindu.

"The Hindu community was infuriated. That same night, more than 1,500 Muslims were killed.

"The next morning, in the same newspaper, on the fifth page, in a small corner, you could see an apology saying that that news had been untrue. And they tendered that apology only because the government had told them, 'Either you prove it, or you must retract.'

"So Shanti Sena has to fight rumors. And the best way to fight rumors is to give correct, unbiased information.

"We immediately go to the place mentioned to check the facts. We have the advantage in this, because very often Shanti Sena is the only group moving within both communities. So, when there is a rumor such as, 'In the Muslim area, they are gathering weapons,' we say, 'Have you been there? We slept there last night. And we know that nothing of the sort is happening.'

"Usually we do not have access to radio or the newspapers, so we have to use alternative means to spread our information. We use megaphones, or hand out mimeographed leaflets, or post messages on the neighborhood blackboards that some of our cities have. There are ten thousand such blackboards in Ahmedabad, and within half an hour the entire city can be given a message."

Both rumors and violence multiply where there is fear, so Shanti Sena works hard to counter it.

"Fear and courage are equally contagious. So Shanti Sainiks often go to areas that are supposed to be dangerous to show that there is nothing to fear.

"For example, in Bhivandi, when we met with the Hindus, they said, 'Why talk to *us* about peace? Why don't you try to go to the Muslim part of the city? The minute you go there, you'll be killed!'

"So we said, 'All right, we'll go lodge there.' Then we went and lived with the Muslims.

"The Hindus of that city were amazed. They could never have imagined that a mostly Hindu group, including five Hindu women, could stay with the Muslims overnight and be alive the next morning. But we were all safe. Not only were *we* safe, but the Muslims thought *they* were safe, because they had Hindu Shanti Sainiks protecting them.

"In Calcutta in 1964, we organized a silent procession of 3,000 people through the streets where there had been violence. This is one of the most effective techniques to fight fear. On all the streets, just as we passed by, the closed shops were thrown open, and the shop owners would say, 'Ah, we are safe now that Shanti Sena has come.'

"Wherever Shanti Sena functions, it creates this atmosphere of trust."

As violence subsides, the Sainiks shift their focus to reconstruction efforts. This often becomes another means to reconcile the opposing communities.

"In the state of Orissa, there was a riot in which the Christians burned down the homes of the Muslims. My mother-in-law and other Shanti Sainiks there persuaded the Christian community to donate funds for rebuilding the Muslims' houses.

Some of the people who contributed were some of the ones who had burned them down!"

According to Narayan, Shanti Sena works under several handicaps. Most of the Sainiks live in rural areas, but the riots are in towns and cities. Shanti Sena lacks quick means of communication and transportation. It sometimes takes two or three days just to get permission to pass through military lines into a city. As a result, Shanti Sena usually arrives only after the worst violence has passed. Most of its success, then, has been in bringing hostilities to a close more rapidly and moving warring communities toward reconciliation.

But there have been times when violence has been averted.

"This is possible when a Shanti Sainik has lived in an area for a long time. The Shanti Sainik would assess the situation and talk to the right people, and in this way prevent a real outbreak. Of course, in a case like this, Shanti Sena would receive no credit, because things would go on as normal, and the public would not know there had been a likelihood of a riot.

"Peace is not news."

Besides combatting riots, Shanti Sena has engaged in relief work during famines and following floods and earthquakes. And in 1971, when violent repression by the Pakistani army forced ten million refugees out of East Pakistan (now Bangladesh), Shanti Sena and other Gandhian groups handled relief operations for 800,000 of the refugees.

◄ ►

Shanti Sena has helped inspire a series of international actions and organizations modeled in part on itself.

In late 1961, 55 activists from thirteen countries (Narayan among them) met near Beirut, Lebanon, and founded the World Peace Brigade. Jayaprakash Narayan was chosen as a cochairman, along with Michael Scott of Britain and A. J. Muste of the United States, both of them prominent Gandhian activists.

For its first action, the brigade planned an international Freedom March into Northern Rhodesia (now Zambia), working jointly with the leader of Northern Rhodesia's nonviolent liberation movement, Kenneth Kaunda. The prospect of this march and of an accompanying general strike helped put pressure on Britain, which finally arranged the elections that brought Kaunda's party to power.

The other most important action of the World Peace Brigade was the 1963 Delhi–Peking Friendship March, following a brief border war between India and China in 1962. The core of the march was a group of seventeen activists from India, England, Austria, Japan, and the United States. Though Shanti Sena organized it, the march was placed under the auspices of the brigade to convey that the action rose above nationalist interests.

"This was a time of war psychosis in India, and it was very difficult for these people to talk about friendship with China," Narayan said. "There were articles written against them and even statements against them in the Indian Parliament. But every place they passed through, they created a favorable atmosphere for peace."

Near each of their daily stops along the route from Delhi to the Chinese border, the core group was joined in their march by hundreds, sometimes thousands of local residents.

"They walked about 2,000 miles, until they reached the far border of India and China—and then the Chinese government would not allow them to enter. But the march had already helped calm the war fever within India itself."

After the Delhi–Peking March, the World Peace Brigade faded away, both because of problems in maintaining a world organization and from simple neglect. (By this time, American activists were completely caught up in the civil rights movement.) But brigade veterans cooperated on later international efforts.

The first was the 1964 Nagaland Peace Mission, led by Jayaprakash Narayan and Michael Scott. Nagaland, a region in the far northeast of India, was where guerrillas were battling the Indian army to gain independence from India for the Naga people. The international peace mission managed to negotiate a ceasefire, which was then monitored over the next eight years by a team of observers headed by Gandhians of India.

"Peace has been restored there ever since," Narayan said.

In 1972, Narayan and other brigade veterans were among those carrying out the Cyprus Resettlement Project. In the civil strife on that Mediterranean island, Greek Cypriots had driven Turkish Cypriots from many villages and destroyed their homes. The Cyprus Resettlement Project aimed at involving both Turkish and Greek Cypriots in rebuilding some of these homes, for the resettlement of Turkish Cypriot refugees.

The activists managed to secure the cooperation of leaders from both sides, and in the process became the first group to get representatives of both sides to sit at the same table for talks on any topic. Joint teams of Greek and Turkish Cypriots had actu- ally begun rebuilding a few homes when the project was cut short by the Turkish army's invasion of the island.

At the time of my India visit, the idea of international peace brigades had remained in limbo for half a decade. But, at the end of the 1970s, the spate of world crises beginning with the Iranian and Afghanistan conflicts set the idea moving once more.

Since then, projects and proposals for international actions have emerged independently from many sources, and brigades have already made their way to Iran, the Middle East, and Cen- tral America.

Among the current initiatives, the one most directly connected to past efforts is Peace Brigades International. Founded in 1981, PBI was partly inspired by a call from Vinoba for a new World Peace Brigade, and it includes a number of WPB veterans. Narayan Desai is a cofounder and has been one of its three to four international directors since its founding. PBI intends to be an international Shanti Sena.

So far, PBI has focused its efforts on Central America. In September 1983, PBI stationed a team for two weeks in a Nica- raguan town near the Honduras border, apparently succeeding in discouraging attacks on the town by United States–backed guerrillas. This Nicaragua mission was a prelude to similar but ongoing efforts by the ad hoc organization Witness for Peace (see chapter 8).

PBI's most important project so far has been the maintenance of a team of three to seven in Guatemala since March 1983, working for reconciliation and human rights. In one instance, 63 Guatemalan Indian women and their children were threat- ened with starvation when a civilian paramilitary patrol prevented them from selling their handcrafts or receiving emergency food donations. The PBI team successfully negotiated a lifting of the ban.

The team in Guatemala has also assisted the Mutual Support Group for Relatives of the Disappeared (GAM), formed in 1984. The group seeks to pressure the government to return relatives believed to have been abducted by the government or by progovernment forces but believed possibly still to be alive. Following the torture and assassination of one GAM leader and the apparent assassination of another leader along with two family members, the PBI team (in conjunction with the U.S. organization Fellowship of Reconciliation) has maintained an escort service for GAM leaders.

In spring 1986, PBI was also organizing training camps in peace army techniques for persons from Sri Lanka and South Africa.

◂ ▸

It would be hard to imagine better training for a nonviolent activist than a stint in the Gandhians' peace army. A chance to test this training in a different setting came to Narayan when his colleague Jayaprakash Narayan (JP) began his movement in Bihar. (The story of JP's movement is told in chapter 2.)

Narayan Desai was involved in the movement almost from its beginning, helping to organize demonstrations in Bihar and working with student groups around the state. In these first months, the government and much of the media were playing up isolated instances of violence by the protesters. But Narayan got a different view.

"I must say, I became an admirer of the young people," he told me. "I never realized they could be so disciplined when tested. Sometimes when they were beaten up, all they would do would be to raise their arms to shield themselves."

During one march, 22 demonstrators were injured by pellets fired from the house of a Congress party legislator.

"There were 100,000 young people who could have set fire to the building from which the firing came," Narayan said. "But, instead, they just stood on the road shouting, 'No matter how severe the attack, we will not raise our hands against it.' "

Later, Narayan had reason to learn similar respect for the wider body of JP's supporters. JP was at one point planning a three-day statewide general strike, during which nearly all normal activity would be halted. Narayan was sent around Bihar to check conditions for the strike.

One of the planned actions was for people to sit on railroad tracks to stop trains. But Narayan found that some of JP's politician supporters were calling for people to pull up the tracks. "So I advised JP not to include the stopping of trains, because some people might pull up tracks—and the government was too keen to seize on something like that to prove that our movement was violent."

Despite Narayan's urgent arguments, JP refused to change the plans, saying, "I have faith that the people will not be violent."

Narayan finally deferred to JP's judgment, although he remained unconvinced. But JP proved right: During the strike, people simply sat in large crowds on the tracks, stopping all trains, without pulling up tracks.

The first two days of the strike passed without serious incident, while regular activity came to a virtual halt throughout the state. The capital city of Patna, where JP and Narayan were stationed, was like a dead city. During the second night, though, a phone call came to JP's headquarters from the office of the chief minister (the Indian equivalent of a state governor). "A friend in that office used to tell us everything that was happening," Narayan told me, with one of his ironic smiles.

The friend related that a meeting was in progress between top police and government officials, including the chief minister himself. They were all very concerned that two days of the strike had passed peacefully; and the chief minister had said in effect, "Tomorrow, by any means, there must be violence, or our cause is lost." How to provoke the violence was the question then being considered.

The next morning, Narayan was helping to oversee a nonviolent blockade of the state legislature. JP arrived a little later to lead the picketing, after having ridden by jeep around Patna warning against provocation by government forces.

Suddenly a police officer arrived with a message from the chief minister. He told JP, "The Patna City Railway Station is burning, and there is violence there—just for your information."

Narayan had been working with the people near that railway station, so JP asked him to go at once and check out the story. Narayan borrowed JP's jeep and, taking the obliging officer along to get him behind police lines, rushed off to Patna City Station.

As they approached the station, Narayan could hear gunshots. The road to the station ran along the top of a ridge; and when they got closer, he saw people running up one side of the ridge, throwing rocks at police on the other side, and running back down before the police could fire.

When the jeep reached near the crowd, Narayan at once left the jeep, ran down to the rock-throwers, and began scolding them. "What are you doing? This is not the way to run our movement! We have pledged to keep it peaceful!"

But people in the crowd said, "Why talk to *us* about nonviolence? They're the ones who started firing. Why don't you go talk to *them?*"

Narayan said, "I have come to do exactly that, but I can't talk to them unless you stop throwing rocks."

So the crowd agreed to stop for a while. Narayan then rushed over the ridge to the police side and asked to see the officer in charge. The police told him that the officer, a district magistrate named Dubey (pronounced Doo-bay), was on the other side of the railway station; but one of them led Narayan to a police jeep, where he could talk to Dubey by radio.

Just as Narayan came up to the jeep, a message was coming over the radio. It was Dubey calling his headquarters. Narayan heard Dubey saying, "The Patna City Station is burning, and my forces are not enough to control the crowd. Please send reinforcements."

Now, Narayan was standing right next to the railway station. There was no fire.

He waited a few minutes more, so Dubey wouldn't know he had overheard; then he asked the policeman to tell Dubey he wanted to come meet with him. He heard Dubey first tell the policeman not to let Narayan come, then change his mind and permit it.

Narayan walked across the railway station to where Dubey stood.

When he saw Narayan, Dubey began to upbraid him. "Is this what you call nonviolence, Narayanbhai (Brother Narayan)? Just look what is happening!"

Some distance down the tracks, Narayan could see some people throwing rocks at police; and about a quarter mile along, a signal cabin was burning. So that was the "Patna City Station burning"!

Narayan turned to Dubey and said, "Mr. Dubey, I have not come here to debate violence and nonviolence. I have come to see things for myself. But I must also say to you, you seem very excited. You are at the point where no one can do things properly. What has made you so excited?" Taking advantage of his greater age to play "elder brother" (a tactic perhaps better suited to India than to the West), Narayan put his hand on Dubey's shoulder, patted him a little, and tried to quiet him down.

Dubey began to look a bit sheepish, and finally said, "What can we do?"

Narayan said, "Let me try."

Dubey thought for a moment, then said, "All right. I will give you five minutes to stop this rock-throwing."

Next Narayan needed a way to approach the crowd without seeming to be from the police. He quickly got Dubey's permission to use the loudspeaker system in Dubey's jeep. He began shouting over it, "Long live People's Leader Jayaprakash"— "Loknayak Jayaprakash, zindabad, zindabad." The third time he shouted "Loknayak Jayaprakash," the crowd answered, "Zindabad, zindabad."

The connection Narayan needed had been made, and he at once set off to meet the crowd.

As he approached along the tracks, some of the people in the crowd recognized him and told the others they must listen to Narayan, as JP's lieutenant. As before, Narayan admonished the crowd. "Why are you doing this? This is not the right way!"

"But they have been firing on us!" replied some in the crowd. "They have already killed many people!"

"I wish to see the bodies," said Narayan. "Where are they?"

"In the village, nearby."

"Come then," said Narayan, "let's see them. I don't want to depend on hearsay."

He began moving the crowd along the tracks, back toward the village. He needed to get the facts straight on whatever violence there had been. Even more important, he had to draw the crowd away from the station and *keep* it away.

As Narayan and the villagers passed by the burning signal cabin, some of the villagers raised an alarm and pointed behind. A photographer, apparently sent by Dubey, was trying to get a picture of Narayan and the crowd next to the burning cabin! Narayan fiercely scolded the photographer, telling him to go back at once. The photographer was so taken aback that he turned around and went back without his picture.

But Dubey had yet to play his last card.

As Narayan's group got closer to the village, with Narayan a few steps behind the others, some of the people suddenly turned and started throwing rocks in his direction.

Bewildered, Narayan said, "Why are you throwing rocks at me?"

People in the crowd said, "No, no, look behind you."

What Narayan didn't realize was that Dubey and six riflemen had come up behind. When the crowd started throwing rocks at them, that was all the excuse Dubey needed. Before Narayan could even turn around to look, he heard the commands: "Attention . . . . On your mark . . . . "

Narayan knew what the third command would be. At that moment he was standing between the crowd and the police, about 6 feet from the rifles. There wasn't much doubt who would be among the first to be shot.

With no time to think, Narayan whirled toward Dubey and shouted:

"What are you doing? Do you want to kill me? I am trying to take the crowd away from the tracks! Please go back at once!"

It worked. Dubey was so taken by surprise that he led the riflemen back toward the station. In fact, he went all the way over to the other side of the station, and after a while began firing on the crowd over there. (The next day, Dubey told the press that JP had sent his lieutenant to the railway station, but the lieutenant had been unable to control the crowd.)

Meanwhile, on the way to the village, Narayan was discovering that the crowd had used the word "killed" somewhat loosely. When he asked, "Where are the dead?" someone would show a wound and say, "Not dead, but look, they have killed *me!*" (Narayan, though, did eventually see two dead bodies, as well as many injuries, and at least one injured person died later.)

Once they got to the village, Narayan began talking to the crowd to try to divert the people from the idea of returning to the tracks. But one villager challenged him, asking him to lead them back to sit on the tracks peacefully, as had been called for in the strike program.

Narayan told them, "I won't lead you there, nor do I want you to go, because the police will use this as an excuse to come down to this village and shoot innocent people. But, if you like, I can instead hear the story of what happened, and go and report it immediately to Jayaprakash."

The villagers said, "Yes, we would like you to report to Jayaprakash."

"Then, there is one condition," Narayan told them. "Until he and I come back, you won't return to the tracks."

The villagers agreed, and began to tell their story to Narayan, who took quick notes. It seemed clearly a case of the police starting to fire on the crowd while they sat peacefully on the tracks; the stone-throwing apparently had come only after that. (This was later confirmed by a reliable source.)

Not so strangely, as Narayan had already seen, the police had come with photo equipment. Later, a movie was made of the incident, which was shown all across India to illustrate the violence used by the protesters in Bihar. Narayan's report, though, helped to establish a different view in a formal inquiry into the case set up by JP.

◄ ►

Not long after the general strike, the government began expelling the top Gandhian leaders from the state. JP asked Narayan to go underground as a standby, in case JP himself was arrested.

Then, after the dramatic November 4 rally in Patna, it looked as if the government might ease up on security measures. So Narayan came into the open.

He was at once served with an externment order and escorted out of state.

After that, following JP's instructions, Narayan stayed outside Bihar, touring several states to give talks on the movement.

Then came JP's arrest and Indira Gandhi's declaration of a national emergency. Narayan was sitting at breakfast on the porch of his house at Sarva Seva Sangh headquarters when the announcement came over the radio.

Narayan knew that if he wanted to escape arrest he would have to leave at once. But it happened that everyone in his immediate family was then seriously ill, so he was reluctant to go.

His wife, Uttara, though, told him, "No matter how much you want to stay with us, the government is not likely to oblige you."

Within ten minutes of the announcement, Narayan had quietly fled Sarva Seva Sangh.

He stayed that day at the home of a friend. That evening, a police superintendent, a friend of Narayan's host, came by to warn the host to keep a low profile. When the host confided to the officer that Narayan was hiding there, the officer said, "They are due here to search for him within the hour!"

The two of them bundled Narayan into the officer's car, and the officer drove off.

As they rode, the officer told Narayan, "We have been preparing for these arrests for the past half year. We all have our lists of people to arrest, and you are on one of them. But I'm willing to help you, Narayanbhai, because I know you would never encourage violence."

He dropped Narayan off at a railway station, then went off to arrest the people on his own list.

Narayan headed toward his native state of Gujarat in western India, which was relatively safe at the time, since opposition political parties controlled the state government. Once there, Narayan moved among several cities before finally settling in the capital city of Ahmedabad.

During this early period, Narayan attended a secret gathering with George Fernandes, head of the Socialist party and later Janata cabinet member, who was also in hiding. Fernandes was the expected leader of any major resistance there might be to Indira Gandhi's government. (The Gandhians could not be a substantial force, since most of those active in the JP Movement were in jail.)

Fernandes told the people gathered that he was prepared to use violence. "My hero is not the JP of 1975," he said, "but the JP of 1942"—the year JP had attempted to organize sabotage and armed resistance against the British. Then Fernandes turned to Narayan and asked what he thought.

Narayan said, "It will isolate the movement and make it easy to crush. Violence is counterrevolutionary."

Whether or not Fernandes was influenced by Narayan's answer, he organized no violent resistance.

Meanwhile, Narayan was learning his own lessons from the Emergency. At a party in one city, he ran into some members of the Congress party who knew him and who plied him with questions about his future plans. Narayan managed to evade their queries. But secrecy is not a virtue in the Gandhian philosophy, and Narayan felt uneasy about having resorted to it.

Another practice, too, caused him uneasiness. Narayan had grown a mustache as a sort of disguise. When he reached Ahmedabad, a friend chided him for it, telling him, "This is not very Gandhian."

Narayan finally decided that his safety was not worth compromising himself morally through secrecy and deceit. The mustache came off, and Narayan hid no longer, becoming instead active and visible in his opposition to the Emergency.

Narayan began writing signed articles criticizing the government, for publication in a regional Gandhian journal called *Bhoomiputra* (*Son of the Soil*). The publishers of this journal had decided soon after the declaration of emergency to defy censorship and continue their criticism of the government until ordered to shut down. But because of sheer bureaucratic inertia, the government's response came much more slowly than expected.

When the government finally did take official action, the

publishers managed to counter with assertions that they were abiding by the censorship laws. These laws prohibited publishing anything that would hurt the "peace and unity" of the country—which the publishers insisted they as Gandhians would never do.

Through the publishers' determination to face up to government harassment, *Bhoomiputra* became a national symbol of fearless journalism.

Besides his articles, Narayan wrote a number of booklets. One of them, *The Nature of Dictatorship*, stayed within the law by not mentioning Indira Gandhi or even India, though anyone could tell how it was meant to apply. Another was *The Story of Resistance*, with examples of effective nationwide nonviolent resistance from Czechoslovakia (against the Soviet Union) and Norway (against the Nazis). Both booklets were eventually banned—but not before each had gone through three printings.

It happened that 1975 was the centennial of the birth of Sardar Patel, a close colleague of Gandhi in the struggle for independence and later an important government leader. Narayan and others organized a month-long march across Gujarat in honor of the centennial. The marchers stopped for three mass meetings a day and spoke openly against the Emergency.

Finally, Indira Gandhi used a feature of the Indian Constitution to impose national control over Gujarat. After that, government repression in Gujarat was even worse than elsewhere in India.

Undaunted, Narayan began publishing his own national newsletter, with a circulation of 3,000. It came out regularly for five issues, until workers at the press grew afraid of arrest and refused to print it. After that, Narayan ran off the newsletter on a mimeo machine in the form of a signed letter, publishing several more issues before running out of funds.

Though there were many underground papers published during the Emergency, Narayan's was unusual in two ways: It carried reliable news that was not common knowledge, and it bore the name of the author/publisher. Narayan found that signing his statements gave them much more weight, because people could see he was risking arrest to make them.

"One of the things an oppressor does is to terrorize," Narayan

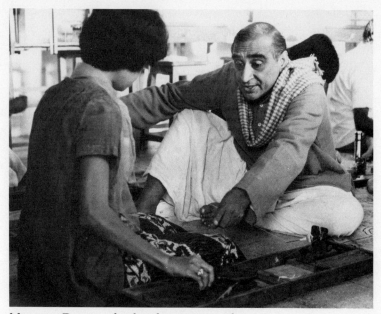

Narayan Desai and a hand-spinning student

said. "So we must become detached and willing to lose all. Then terror has no hold."

For Narayan, these years—and his work with Shanti Sena—had provided many opportunities to learn such fearlessness.

◄►

Since my visit to India, Narayan has moved his home from Sarva Seva Sangh headquarters in Benares to his native state of Gujarat. There he has founded the Institute for Total Revolution, where he devotes himself to training a new generation of Gandhian activists. He is also increasingly called overseas, where he shares his knowledge of peace soldiering and other aspects of Gandhian activism.

But whatever changes come in Narayan's life, there is one thing unlikely to change.

He is still spinning.

4 "*Hug the Trees!*"

Earth provides enough to satisfy every man's need, but not every man's greed.

◄ Gandhi

At the time of my India visit, I knew next to nothing about the rapid destruction of forests in Third World countries, or about its costs in terms of firewood shortage, soil erosion, weather shifts, and famine. Still, I was at once intrigued at hearing about the Chipko Movement—mountain villagers stopping lumber companies from clear-cutting mountain slopes by issuing a call to "hug the trees."

So one morning—along with a Gandhian friend, a young engineer—I found myself on the bus out of Rishikesh, following the river Ganges toward its source.

Before long we had left the crowded plains behind and were climbing into the Himalayas. Thick forest covered the mountain slopes, interrupted only occasionally by terraced fields reaching dramatically up the mountainsides. Our bus bumped along a winding road halfway between the river below and the peaks above, as it followed the river's meanders around the sides of mountains.

This was the Uttarakhand—the name given to the Himalayas of Uttar Pradesh state, lying against India's border with Chinese-ruled Tibet. A major source of timber and water power, this was a region of vast natural riches—in contrast to the poverty of the people living there.

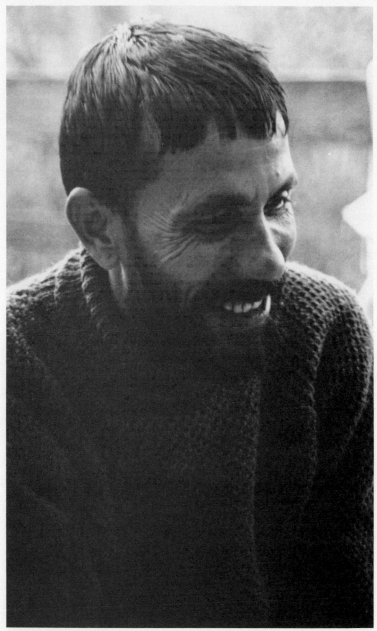

Chandi Prasad Bhatt

Yet even the forest riches of the Uttarakhand might have their limits. After an hour or two of the ride, the forests within sight of the road were becoming noticeably thinner. Still later we could see deep gashes running up the sides of the mountains. "Landslides," my friend explained.

At some points the bus came upon debris piled up at the edges of the road; and several times the bus had to drive over debris not yet cleared away. The slopes were increasingly bare.

It was completely dark when we spotted the lights of the small town of Gopeshwar, birthplace of the Chipko Movement. There we would hear that movement's story from its founder, Chandi Prasad Bhatt.

◄ ►

Chandi Prasad Bhatt was raised in Gopeshwar—a very small village, during his youth. Farmland was scarce in the over-populated mountains, and so were jobs. Like most men of the mountain villages, Chandi Prasad was eventually forced to work in the plains, becoming a ticket clerk in Rishikesh for the bus company.

Chandi Prasad felt deeply concerned over the plight of the mountain people as a whole, and he often walked through the mountains to talk to the villagers about their problems. Among the most important, of course, were the shortages in farmland and jobs. But added to these were oppressive government poli-cies concerning the forests.

The villagers depended on the forests for firewood, fodder for their cattle, and wood for their houses and farm tools. But the government restricted huge areas of forest from their use, and then auctioned off the trees to lumber companies and industries from the plains—a practice inherited with little change from the British colonialists. Because of these restrictions and an ever-growing population, the mountain women found themselves walking hours each day just to gather firewood and fodder.

In 1956, Chandi Prasad found hope when he heard a speech by Jayaprakash Narayan, who was on a tour of the area. Chandi Prasad and other young people launched themselves into the

Sarvodaya Movement, organizing Bhoodan and Gramdan and fighting liquor abuse throughout the Uttarakhand.

Then, in 1962, a brief border war between India and China brought drastic change to the Uttarakhand. Though the region had not itself been involved in the conflict, the Indian government wanted to secure more tightly all its territory bordering China. For the Uttarakhand, this entailed a program of rapid economic development.

Road-building began throughout the region. Lumbering operations escalated as the roads brought remote forests into easier reach. Towns grew as workers arrived from the plains.

The mountain people didn't benefit much from this development, though they were meant to. Construction work was assigned to contractors from the plains, who brought with them skilled and semiskilled laborers. The mountain people themselves were hired only for jobs such as hauling rocks, and were paid next to nothing. Meanwhile, the increase in population and lumbering made it even harder for the mountain women to find their firewood and fodder.

Chandi Prasad and other Sarvodaya workers decided to tackle the problem of job discrimination. They organized a labor cooperative, with 30 full-time members and 700 part-time, which bid for and won several contracts to build sections of road. On these jobs, the co-op was able to pay double the wages paid by outside contractors to their own workers.

But the co-op soon found hurdles placed in its way. For instance, its completed jobs were undervalued by government assessors, causing the co-op to lose money. It seemed the co-op's practices and success had offended some people. The co-op was faced with the choice of either losing more money or greasing the palms of government officials. Instead, it decided to stop building roads.

The workers formed a new organization, the Dasholi Gram Swarajya Sangh, with the aim of starting small industries using the resources of the forests. Its first project was a small workshop making farm tools for local use.

After a while, the workers decided to bid for trees from the local forests. Large lots of trees were sold by the state Forest

Department through the "contractor system," which awarded the trees to the highest bidder, with the purchase price going to the state government. Sometimes the Forest Department sold selected trees, marked for felling; at other times, it sold the rights to a marked area, which was then clear-cut. Normally the contracts went to large businesses from the plains, which took the trees to the plains for sale and for factory use.

With money borrowed from the community, the Sangh over time bid for and won four small contracts, selling some of the wood locally and the rest in the plains. Within a few years the number of full-time workers in the Sangh had increased from 30 to over 200.

But the big contractors seemed determined to halt the competition. They began to overbid on the contracts, while making up their losses by illegally cutting extra trees. Again the workers were forced to turn elsewhere.

The workers had better luck with a plan to buy and market herbs collected by mountain gatherers—herbs that were normally sold to plains traders, who made exaggerated profits on resale. The Sangh was able to pay much higher prices to the gatherers, and even drove up the prices paid by other traders.

Encouraged by this success, the Sangh next built a small processing plant to make resin and turpentine from pine sap—one of eight such processing plants being set up in the region with help from the federal government. But again the Sangh ran into discrimination, when the state Forest Department refused to allot adequate supplies of pine sap to the eight plants, or to allow the plants to buy the sap at the same price paid by a partly government-owned producer in the plains.

In 1970, the workers encountered another consequence of official forest policy—this one more grim than any they had faced before.

During that year's monsoon rain, the Alakhnanda River rose 60 feet, flooding hundreds of square miles. The waters swept away hundreds of homes—including one entire village—as well as 30 passenger-laden buses and five major bridges. Almost 200 people died. When the waters reached the plains, over 100 miles downstream, they dropped silt that clogged nearly 100 miles of canal, halting irrigation and power production in the northern part of the state for six months before the residue could be cleared.

Workers from the Sangh mounted a relief operation for mountain villages marooned by the flood. During the operation, the workers tried to discover what had caused the flood, by talking to the villagers and making their own observations. It became clear that this disaster was not strictly natural.

The chief cause, the Sangh workers decided, was the commercial lumbering that had expanded so dramatically after the war with China. When mountain slopes were cleared of trees, rains washed away the topsoil, leaving the soil and rocks underneath to crumble and fall, in landslides. Much of the soil from the mountain slopes was deposited in the rivers below, raising the water level and forming temporary dams that could burst under pressure. At the same time, the bare slopes allowed much more rain to run off directly into the river. The end result was floods.

Forest Department officials allotted trees without regard to these effects, which they didn't seem aware of. On top of that, contractors regularly bribed the forest rangers to let them take trees beyond their allotment. The Forest Department had a program of replanting cleared slopes, but it was inadequate; so bare slopes usually remained bare.

Another cause contributing to floods was road building, which often resulted in landslides when proper construction methods were neglected.

The mountain people themselves were not blameless. They had bared many slopes while gathering firewood and fodder and while grazing their livestock, either not realizing or not caring much about the effects of their actions. Of course, they were forced to meet their survival needs from areas limited by the government—which became harder to do as the population grew. Besides that, the government policies made the villagers feel the forests did not belong to them—that the government merely allowed them to live there—which discouraged any sense of responsibility the villagers might have for preserving the forests.

The Sangh workers prepared a report of their findings and

submitted it to the government. It brought no response. But the workers themselves had learned a lesson they would not forget: The same forest policy that denied them fair use of forest resources was gradually destroying their mountain home.

◄ ►

In October 1971, the Sangh workers held a demonstration in Gopeshwar to protest the policies of the Forest Department. They demanded that the department abolish the contractor system and instead award contracts to local cooperatives—to generate jobs for the mountain people while halting the contractors' illegal felling practices. They also demanded an end to discrimination in the supply of pine sap, and enough access to the forests so that the mountain people could meet their needs.

Over the next year, the Sangh workers pressed their demands through a press campaign and talks with high officials. None of this seemed to bear fruit. In late 1972, more rallies and marches were held, but these too failed to bring results. The thoughts of the Sangh workers turned toward direct action.

Meanwhile, the Sangh received a fresh blow: The Forest Department turned down the Sangh's annual request for ash trees for its farm tools workshop. The department then allotted some of the same ash trees to the Simon Company, a sporting goods manufacturer from the plains. Tennis rackets took priority over plows!

In March 1973, two Simon Company agents arrived in Gopeshwar to supervise the cutting of the trees. Told there was no hotel, they applied for lodging at the guest rooms of—the Dasholi Gram Swarajya Sangh.

When the agents told the Sangh workers who they were and what their business was in town, the workers were stunned. But they quickly remembered their traditional hospitality and helped the visitors settle into their rooms. Then they rushed off to tell Chandi Prasad Bhatt.

The news hit Chandi Prasad hard. He declared, "Let them know we will not allow the felling of a single tree. When their men raise their axes, we will embrace the trees to protect them."

A few days later, a public meeting was held in the courtyard of the Sangh compound to discuss the situation. A number of ideas were advanced: barring entrance to the forest, stopping the truck from hauling away trees by lying in front of it, cutting the trees ahead of time, or even burning them.

Finally, Chandi Prasad said, "Our aim is not to destroy the trees but to preserve them. When the men go to cut them, why don't we cling to the trees, and dare them to let their axes fall on our backs?" (*Chipko* means "hug," or "cling to.") As he described it, he locked his hands together in a posture of embrace.

The people were at first stunned by the novelty of the idea. Then they began to shout their agreement: Yes, they would hug the trees! They drew up a resolution announcing their plan, to be sent to government officials. The Simon Company agents, who had been allowed into the meeting, watched in consternation.

Several weeks later, the Sangh workers learned that the trees were marked and were about to be felled. On the appointed day, Sangh workers and others marched in procession out of Gopeshwar toward Mandal forest, where the marked trees stood. Accompanied by the beat of drums, they sang traditional songs voicing their concern for their natural home. When they reached Mandal village, just below the forest, a rally of about 100 people was held.

The lumbermen were already in the forest waiting for their employers. The Simon Company agents had collected their final permit from officials in Gopeshwar and were on their way to the forest. But when they reached Mandal village, they were so unnerved to see the animated crowd, they abandoned their plans and withdrew without the trees!

Following this, Forest Department officials tried to bargain with the Sangh workers: The Sangh could have one ash tree if it allowed the Simon Company its full quota. The Sangh refused.

The officials raised the offer to two ash trees; then three; then five. Finally, the offer reached ten trees—the Sangh's original request.

But the Sangh workers were unwilling to allow the Simon Company its quota at *any* price. The issue was no longer only whether the Sangh would get trees for its farm tools workshop.

At issue now was an entire government forest policy more concerned about outside businesses than about the people who lived among the forests. The allotment of trees to the Simon Company was a glaring symbol of that policy's injustice.

Finally, the government gave in. The Simon Company's permit was canceled, and the trees were assigned to the Sangh instead.

Soon after, the government also announced it was ending the discrimination in pine sap supplies. But that same month, the Sangh workers learned that the Simon Company had been allotted a new set of ash trees, in the Phata forest, in another part of the district.

Chandi Prasad and another worker rushed to the Phata area to tell the villagers about the Simon Company's plans and about the new Chipko Movement. The villagers formed an action committee and set up a continuous watch over the approach to the forest. Simon Company agents had already reached the area, and they watched these preparations. After a few days, they once again retreated from the scene.

But the company wasn't ready to give up the trees, and its permit was good for six months.

In December, more Simon Company employees arrived in Phata with a new strategy. They visited all the villages in the area, threatening the villagers with harsh treatment by the law if they tried to stop the tree-felling. They also claimed that the Chipko leaders were only interested in bribes from the company.

The Simon Company agents were invited to present their viewpoint at a rally called by Chipko leaders. With Chandi Prasad sitting by, the agents tried to intimidate the mountain people with threats and insults. But it was no use. The villagers declared they would protect the trees.

As the rally ended, word spread that the government was showing a movie that night in a nearby town. A movie is a special treat for the mountain people; so, that evening, many of the villagers and Chipko workers went into town to see it. But when they arrived, they found out the film van hadn't come, and the movie had been canceled. They were then stuck in town for the night, since the mountain buses didn't run so late.

When they returned next morning, they were alarmed to hear that men with axes and saws had been seen heading toward the forest.

The Chipko leaders quickly organized a procession, which marched toward the forest to the beat of drums. When the villagers reached the forest, they found that the lumbermen had run away—but had left behind five felled ash trees.

The villagers were dismayed to see the fallen trees. But they soon resolved that the Simon Company would not remove the trees from the forest. A round-the-clock vigil was set up.

A few days later, Simon Company employees tried once more to remove the trees, but retreated when they came upon the Chipko people.

After a week's vigilance by the villagers, the Simon Company's permit expired. The company had failed to obtain a single tree.

◀ ▶

Though the Chipko workers were elated by this victory, there was a much greater challenge to come.

A few months earlier, the Sangh workers had had a fresh reminder of the lessons of the Alakhnanda flood. Disastrous flooding had struck the Mandakini, another major river of the region.

Experts and policymakers in the plains were starting to notice that floods from the Himalayas were becoming steadily worse, and some even saw the connection between human actions and these "natural" disasters. But this awareness failed to reach the people managing the forests. The Forest Department knew only how to allot trees according to principles unchanged for a century—principles that protected the forests from the mountain people, not from the administrators.

The Chipko people knew this, but still they were shocked by what came next. Just months after the Mandakini flood, the Forest Department announced an auction of almost 2,500 trees in the Reni forest—a forest overlooking the Alakhnanda River. The lessons of that river's previous flood had been completely ignored.

A Chipko rally

Chandi Prasad quickly set out for the villages in the Reni area.

In one village, a gathering he spoke to faced the mountain where the forest was to be cut, its peak already ravaged by tree-felling and landslides. Chandi Prasad reminded the villagers of the flood of 1970. He asked if there wouldn't be more landslides and worse floods once the remaining forests on the mountain were cut down.

The villagers nodded agreement. But one of them rose and said they themselves had just marked those trees for the Forest Department.

Chandi Prasad was dismayed. "In that case," he told them, "you might as well have cut the trees yourselves."

The villagers protested: The government had paid them to do it. How could they refuse?

Chandi Prasad said, "And if the government paid you to cut down the trees, would you do that too?"

There was a silence. Then one of the villagers said, "No, we would not cut down the trees. But how can we stop others?"

To their amazement, Chandi Prasad explained that they could save the forest by hugging the trees. After more talk, the villagers agreed.

And so did villagers in other places Chandi Prasad visited. After he left the area, two of his colleagues living there continued to spread the message of Chipko.

The auction was scheduled for the beginning of January in Dehra Dun, a city in the plains. Chandi Prasad went to Dehra Dun shortly before the auction. First he contacted Forest Department officials. He told them about the danger of landslides and floods from cutting the forest, and he pleaded with them to cancel the auction. The officials ignored him.

Chandi Prasad next appealed to the contractors' agents gathering in the city. He warned them that the winning contractor would have to face the resistance of the Chipko Movement. The agents refused to take him seriously. They had heard about the Chipko Movement—but it was one thing to protect a few ash trees, and another to save a whole forest!

The only people who gave Chandi Prasad a sympathetic hearing were a group of students, who proposed to disrupt the auction. But Chandi Prasad couldn't approve such methods. So the students instead printed leaflets and posted them around the auction hall. On the morning of the auction, Chandi Prasad stood at the door of the auction hall and pointed to a posted leaflet as the contractors' agents entered the hall. But their response was the same as before.

At the end of the auction, Chandi Prasad told an employee of the winning contractor that his company would face the Chipko Movement at Reni. Then he returned to Gopeshwar.

Over the next few months, gatherings and rallies were held throughout the Reni area to prepare the people for what was to come.

In mid-March, the first group of contractors' laborers arrived in a town close by the Reni forest to wait for a final permit to enter the area. The villagers and Chipko workers waited tensely for the confrontation.

A week later, government officials made a surprise announcement: Compensation for land taken over for military purposes after the China war would be paid out in Chamoli, a town some distance from Reni. The morning after the announcement, the Reni men rushed to Chamoli to collect their money. After all, they had been pressing for payment for fourteen years! Meanwhile, Chandi Prasad—who had not heard about the announcement—was being held up in Gopeshwar by a visit from a high-level Forest Department official, who had developed a sudden interest in the Dasholi Gram Swarajya Sangh.

That morning, the contractors' men, along with forest officials and a company agent, climbed onto a rented bus and were driven from the town toward Reni forest. Shutters were drawn over the bus windows so no one could see in—though the departure of the village men had left most of the valley deserted. The bus stopped short of the village of Reni, and the men took a roundabout path to avoid the village.

But a little girl spotted the men marching toward the forest and ran to tell Gaura Devi, an elderly leader of the village women. Gaura Devi rushed around the village, calling the other women away from their cooking. Within minutes, about 30 women and children were hurrying toward the forest.

They soon caught up with the men, who had made camp and were preparing lunch. The women pleaded with them not to cut down the forest and explained what it would mean to the village if they did. They asked the men to return to the village after finishing their meal and wait to talk to the village men.

Some of the men seemed ready to respond to the women's pleas; but others had been drinking. The drunk ones tried to take liberties with the women, or cursed at them for trying to interfere with their work.

One of the drunks came staggering toward the women with a gun. Gaura Devi stood in front of him, bared her breast, and said, "This forest is like our mother. You will have to shoot me before you can cut it down."

At this, the sober men decided they had best leave. They

Gaura Devi

Photo by Anupam Mishra

started back down the path out of the forest, while the women kept up their appeal to the drunken ones. Meanwhile, the women spotted a new batch of laborers moving up the path with bags of rations. Some of the women ran to meet them and pleaded with them to go back. The laborers agreed to leave the ration bags where they were and to leave the forest once they had finished the meal prepared for them. They were soon on their way back.

Finally, the drunken men began to sober up and realized there were very few of them left in the forest. They too started back, with the women helping to carry their tools, some distance behind.

At one spot in the path, there was a concrete slab bridging a gap left by a previous landslide. After passing over the slab, the women used the laborers' tools to dislodge it and send it crashing down the slope, cutting off access to the forest.

All night the women sat by the severed end of the path, holding vigil over the forest above and the men huddling by their ration bags below.

The next morning the village men and Chipko workers arrived by bus. They had already learned about the government's deceit and then about the women's surprise victory. Chandi Prasad assured the frightened company men and forest officials that the villagers meant them no harm but only wanted to protect their forest.

The women told the village men their story; but, at this point, they didn't mention the drunkenness of some of the men, or about the gun. After all, they didn't want the offenders to lose their jobs.

◄ ►

Over the next month, rallies were held at the site, and a con-stant watch was kept over the forest. Meanwhile, the mountain women's story caught the attention of the Indian public and created an outcry for the protection of the Reni forest. The government responded to all this with official protests to the Chipko workers and public denunciations of the movement.

But finally Chandi Prasad was called to the state capital to meet with the chief minister. The chief minister agreed to set up a committee of experts to investigate the situation. When this was announced, the contractor withdrew his men from Reni to wait for the committee's decision.

The committee took over two years to finish its report—but its findings were even better than the Chipko workers had at first hoped they might be. The committee said that the Reni forest was a "sensitive area," and that *no* trees should be cut—not only in the Reni forest but also in a larger section of the Alakhnanda watershed that included Reni.

On the basis of the report, the government put a ten-year ban on all tree-felling in an area of over 450 square miles.

The victory at Reni has been followed by other successes. In 1977, the Chipko workers learned that forests were being auctioned in an area next to the one protected by the government ban. They asked the Forest Department to send representatives along with Chipko workers to inspect the region. They also warned the department that a Chipko campaign would be launched if the department failed to take account of what it found there. Following the investigation, another 100 square miles were added to the protected area.

In 1978, Forest Department officials reversed the order of events: They informed Chandi Prasad that they wanted to auction trees in two forests in other parts of the district. They asked him to inspect the forests and tell them if their plans were all right. At the time of my visit, it looked likely that this would lead to protection for another 40 square miles of forest.

Since 1975, the Chipko workers have been not only protecting forest slopes, but restoring bare ones as well. By 1981, over a million trees had been planted through their efforts. Besides the local and immediate benefits, this reforestation has been helping to determine what trees and planting techniques might work best in the region as a whole.

The Chipko workers were also trying to develop methods of forest farming, both to conserve the forests and to create employment. In all these efforts, they were paying special attention to involving the mountain villagers themselves in the care of the trees.

◄ ►

The Chipko Movement has sprouted "branches" in most of the districts of the Uttarakhand, and it seemed likely to spread to other regions as well. Conditions like those in the Uttarakhand are found throughout the Himalayas, both in India and in neighboring countries.

"We hope that movements like ours will slow the deterioration of the mountains and let people know the need to change cutting policies," Chandi Prasad told me. But he believed it would take a massive reforestation effort—funded and coordinated by the national government over decades—to save the Indian Himalayas as a home and source of forest resources.

Such an effort is vital not only to the mountain people but also to those in the plains. India has a critical shortage of trees nationwide and must rely on the Himalayan forests as a permanent source of wood and wood products. Also, floods in the plains, fed by waters from the Himalayas, are becoming more and more severe. (Shortly before my arrival in India, Bihar and surrounding areas were hit by the worst flood in India's recorded history—thousands of people killed, a million homes destroyed, and millions of acres of farmland covered with sand. The waters came from the Himalayas.)

These issues are vital—yet, as Chandi Prasad stressed to me, Chipko is more than an ecology movement.

"The main goal of our movement," he said, "is not *saving* trees, but the *judicious use* of trees."

In a general sense, the Chipko Movement stood for the basic right of a community to control and benefit from the resources of its own home. Although three decades had passed since India had been a colony, the Uttarakhand was still treated as one.

So the Chipko Movement continued to press for a complete remaking of forest policy. Besides the protection of sensitive mountain slopes, it demanded that the resources of the mountain forests benefit the mountain people, by providing jobs and supplying survival needs. What's more, it insisted that the mountain people be given an active role in managing their own forests.

Not that the movement wanted to reserve all benefits of the forests for the mountain people. "We respect the needs of people in the plains for the products of our forests," Chandi Prasad said. But the Chipko people believed that even those needs could be better met if the forests were managed by those who lived among the forests and cared for them.

Outside control of the Uttarakhand's resources had led to their irresponsible use and gradual destruction. In the end, the issues of ecology and community right to resources were closely intertwined.

There was yet one more element to the Chipko Movement that Chandi Prasad wanted to point out: a concern over the basic direction of modern society, over its relentless drive toward progress at any price.

"Our movement goes beyond the erosion of the land, to the erosion of human values," he said.

"The center of all this is humankind. If we are not in a good relationship with the environment, the environment will be destroyed, and we will lose our ground. But if you halt the erosion of humankind, humankind will halt the erosion of the soil."

5 The People's Court

The true practice of law is to unite parties riven asunder.

◄ Gandhi

The girl sat cross-legged on the ground, a long scarf pulled over her head to hide her face. She was sixteen years old, as was the boy sitting beside her.

She wanted a divorce.

After three years of marriage (the girl said), the boy and his father were mistreating her, making her eat outside the house, and roughing her up. She had had enough.

The man hearing her case was short and stocky, with loose tan clothing and a white kerchief over his hair. He sat at a small wooden table with papers spread on it, in the shade of a large tree at one edge of a raised-earth platform. Before him and to the sides of him on the platform, sitting on the ground and facing him, were about 200 *adivasis*—tribal people of an aboriginal race found in many parts of India.

The man gently pointed out to the girl that the boy wanted her to return home to him. "Will you go back and try again if he says he won't act that way anymore?"

The girl held firm.

The man pressed her, still gently: "What are *your* conditions? We can fine him, punish him, anything." But the girl remained unmoved.

Finally the man agreed that the marriage should end.

The People's Court

"Is there a problem in returning a dowry?" he asked. There was no dowry in this case, he was told.

"Any children?" No. "Inside?" No.

The girl owned a few things that she had left at the boy's house, and the boy owned a few things the girl had taken away with her. The value was about equal, so the man declared it an even trade.

The man wrote out the decision, and the boy and the girl thumbprinted it. The adivasi villagers gave it official approval with a shout of "Mahatma Gandhi ki jai!" ("Victory to Mahatma Gandhi!") Someone started through the crowd, passing out *jaggery*—chunks of unrefined sugar, the traditional adivasi token of reconciliation.

With that case concluded, the man turned his attention to the two other cases for the afternoon: a dispute between a father and a husband over who should pay a young woman's medical expenses; and another about a saddle that had been borrowed but not returned.

The man was Harivallabh Parikh, and he was presiding over the People's Court.

◀ ▶

Gandhi had always warned his village workers not to get involved in village disputes. But sometimes circumstances call for some bending of the rules.

That's what happened to Harivallabh Parikh.

Harivallabh had been trained in village development work at Gandhi's Sevagram Ashram. Soon after India achieved its independence, Harivallabh decided to find a village to settle in. So he started hiking through a region of eastern Gujarat state populated mostly by adivasis.

After passing through about 200 villages, he stopped at one to restock his supplies.

"I came into the village to buy some grain," he told me, "and sat down at a stone-mill to grind it. It's unusual to see a man hand-grinding, so I soon had a large audience to talk to."

The villagers hoped Harivallabh might set up a shop in their village, so they invited him to settle there. Harivallabh accepted and left to fetch his wife and a few belongings.

Harivallabh Parikh

But while he was gone, local officials and moneylenders learned of his plans. Figuring that this could mean an end to their taking advantage of the uneducated and unorganized adivasis, they threatened the villagers, warning them not to accept the newcomers.

When Harivallabh and his wife arrived a few weeks later, they found that most of the villagers wouldn't even talk to them. They were forced to live in the open under a tree. They spent the first few days singing devotional songs, making friends with the children, and talking with a few brave adults.

Though Harivallabh remembered Gandhi's advice, disputes were mostly what he heard about from the few villagers who would speak to him; so he saw no way to avoid getting involved. Quarrels were common in the villages around there and could easily lead to murder, even over minor matters. There was also much mistreatment of wives by their husbands.

"In the old days, village councils used to settle disputes," Harivallabh said. "But the people lost faith in the councils when they became tools of the corrupt government and police. That was why disputes in this area started getting out of hand."

Meanwhile, modern legal institutions didn't do nearly as good a job of maintaining order and harmony in communities.

Gandhi, himself a lawyer, had been a harsh critic of the legal system introduced by the British. "The lawyers have enslaved India," Gandhi wrote. The lawyers preyed on quarrels, making them worse by dragging them out and by trying to get the most for their clients—all the while draining their clients' cash.

Harivallabh convinced some of the villagers to let him try to settle their disputes. Sometimes he marked a spot equal in distance from the disputants' homes, where they could meet without loss of prestige. He was often able to settle the disputes in a way both sides could accept.

It was from these beginnings that the People's Court grew.

Meanwhile, Harivallabh's patience had won out. The villagers had figured out a way to avoid reprisals on any one family by the moneylenders and officials: They lodged the couple for a short time in each of the village cottages.

A little later, the villagers built the couple a canopy to stay under. Several months after that, Harivallabh got a grant of government land nearby. There he built his ashram—Anand Niketan, "Abode of Joy."

Over 30 years later, Harivallabh was overseeing development of 1,100 adivasi villages, totaling 1½ million people.

But the heart of the program, he said, was still the People's Court.

◄ ►

The People's Court was now the high court of a judiciary system based in the villages.

"Most cases are handled in the new village councils," Harivallabh said. "It's only the cases they find too hard to handle that are sent here." Many of the spectators at the court were village leaders who came to watch each session as a form of training.

In three decades, the People's Court itself had handled over 30,000 cases of all kinds. Most of these were marriage quarrels, with property disputes next in number. But the court also handled criminal cases—assault, theft, even murder.

The People's Court usually met once or twice a month. Between times, complaints were accepted by the secretary of the court, who issued summonses to the people involved.

"Often it's the guilty person who makes the complaint, to keep it out of the government courts," Harivallabh said. Even reluctant villagers usually responded to the court's summonses, since the community expected them to. But not always.

"If someone doesn't turn up in two or three sessions," Harivallabh said, "we send 50 to 100 people to talk to them and persuade them. If that doesn't work, we send 500, or start fasting in front of their house." Eventually the person would come.

When a case came before the court, each side would tell its story, while Harivallabh asked questions. Other witnesses would be called. Then Harivallabh would state how he understood the case, to check that he'd gotten it straight.

If the case was fairly simple, he would then give a judgment. A harder case would be referred to a jury selected from friends of each side. In these cases, Harivallabh would step in only if the jury couldn't reach a decision.

This was the basic order of procedure, but it was followed only loosely. The People's Court was very informal.

The court's judgments, like its summonses, were almost always respected. When they weren't, the villagers enforced them in the same ways.

But these judgments were seldom a great burden on the guilty. They were aimed mainly at giving fair compensation for wrongs and at making peace between the two sides; often they were only token. This was because the court's power to keep peace was based not on the threat of punishment but on the moral pressure of the community, directed by the court.

For the adivasis, the court was a means to quick, efficient justice, without resort to expensive, drawn-out legal proceedings—proceedings that often fueled bitterness and caused great hardship for one or both parties. And because the People's Court was so close at hand, it helped settle conflicts before they got out of control.

"When I arrived, there were two or three murders in this area every week," Harivallabh said. "Now that's down to three or four a year." The rate of marital separations too had dropped.

Finally, the People's Court was a means of social education. Harivallabh used the court to promote high standards of conduct, fair play, justice, and accountability to the community.

As might be expected, the government courts were not always happy about Harivallabh's efforts to take their place—especially in criminal cases. Harivallabh told of a run-in with the government regarding one of the more than 200 murder cases tried by the People's Court.

"A few years back, a villager named Fatu borrowed a pair of chickens from his neighbor Ramji to feed a guest. Later on, Fatu refused to pay back the chickens. There was an argument. Fatu shot Ramji with an arrow and killed him, in front of Ramji's wife."

Fatu rushed to Harivallabh and told him what he had done. The case was brought before the People's Court. "The judgment was that Fatu would farm Ramji's land for the family, until Ramji's son was old enough to handle it. And that Fatu would eat one meal a week with Ramji's family.

"In the beginning, Fatu resisted going over for his meal, because he was afraid to. When he did start going, the family at first served him his meal outside the door. But, gradually, friendly relations were restored."

Of course, none of this was legal. More trouble came when the police learned of the case and arrested Fatu. "But when they brought him to trial, no one came to testify. The police had to explain to the judge that the case had already been settled by the People's Court."

The judge sent for Harivallabh. Harivallabh reasoned with the judge in private: "Ramji was killed. Now you want to kill Fatu. Who will look after the family?" He convinced the judge that Fatu should be let off. So the judge sent for Fatu and told him that when he returned to the court he should claim the killing was self-defense.

Now, even though adivasi custom accepts killing, lying is considered unpardonable. Fatu told the judge he couldn't do it.

The judge turned to Harivallabh for help.

"I would normally consider myself a devotee of Truth," Harivallabh told me. "But in this case, I urged Fatu to go along with the judge."

Fatu was finally persuaded. But, back in the courtroom, the effort proved too much for him. He blurted out that the killing hadn't been self-defense at all and, what's more, that the judge had told him to lie about it!

The judge declared that Fatu must be a madman. He quickly adjourned the court until the next day, when the court would hear the only eyewitness: Ramji's wife.

The next day Ramji's wife took the stand. She told the court that her husband had been killed by a stranger and that Fatu hadn't even been in the village that day. (Harivallabh had supplied her the story.)

"So, Fatu was acquitted. And, since that time, the government hasn't brought to trial any case settled in the People's Court."

◄ ►

Though the government began leaving the People's Court alone, the People's Court did not always leave the government alone. Government officials have themselves sometimes had to answer to the court.

One case involved three forest rangers who were collecting taxes from the adivasis. The rangers were demanding twice what was owed and pocketing half. This was reported to the People's Court, which took statements from the villagers and then sent summonses to the rangers. One ranger came to the court and confessed, returning the money and signing a promise not to take extra money again.

The other two rangers didn't come. When the rangers' superiors refused to take action, Harivallabh handed the story to the newspapers and announced that the adivasis would protest in front of government offices. Soon after this announcement, a high official arrived to look into the court's complaint. As a result, one of the rangers returned the money; the other lost his job.

In a much more serious incident, the body of a murdered boy was found in the field of a village near his own. When the police came to investigate, they lined up the village men and made them crouch on all fours for three days straight, letting them rest only at night. Any man who moved was beaten.

Several nights later, three police returned to the village and demanded to see a young girl said to have been in love with the murdered boy. They took the girl some distance away, and all three raped her. They thrust a stick into her vagina to make her bleed, so there would be no evidence of the rape, then left her bound and gagged. The village women found the girl soon after.

The People's Court was called into special session. When the villagers heard the story, several rose and said they would burn down the police station. The villagers were ready to do it, and Harivallabh himself could hardly contain his anger; but he finally convinced them to take a calmer approach.

Several people were sent to the village to get all the facts in the case. Then Harivallabh and others set the story before a local police official. The official assured them that action would be taken and agreed to meet with the court the next day. But, when he arrived at the court, he brought with him a local businessman and a state legislator, who joined him in asking that the villagers forget the whole affair.

The villagers were not ready to forget it. The story—along with a threat of further action—was sent to the government and to the newspapers, which gave it wide publicity. Following this, the three police who had raped the girl were removed from service.

Still not satisfied, 1,500 of the villagers staged a one-day, 40-mile march to two local government centers. Finally, one of the high-ranking officers involved in the murder investigation was demoted and transferred.

Local businessmen and politicians rushed to the state capital to get the demotion reversed. But the chief minister (equivalent to a state governor) reportedly told them he didn't wish to cut short the life of his administration by letting an adivasi uprising grow to invincible strength.

Harivallabh and the adivasis were demonstrating that almost nothing can stand in the way of a united community. And building unity is what the People's Court is all about.

6 New Dawn Gift-Village

To model an ideal village may be the work of a lifetime.
◄ Gandhi

I would develop in the child his hands, his brain, and his soul. The hands have almost atrophied. The soul has been altogether ignored.
◄ Gandhi

No one else I met in India resembled Radhakrishna Menon. He was tall and gangly, with bushy white hair and busy white eyebrows. When he spoke, he gestured widely; and he often knit his eyebrows as he smiled, in what could only be called a ferocious grin.

When he walked in the lead, he had the extremely annoying habit of halting whenever he spoke, which constantly brought me up short behind him. He frequently was doing this on a sultry January morning in the southern state of Kerala, as he led me on the main path through Navodaya Danagram—"New Dawn Gift-Village." Radhakrishna—this engaging character—was the founder, mentor, and guide of Danagram.

Here, I had been told, I would find the spirit of Gramdan.

We walked between coconut palms and other lush growth, on the central hill of three on which Danagram lay. We passed a couple of pavilionlike community buildings, one of which housed a nursery school and an infant feeding program, both

Radhakrishna Menon

run by the village women's organization. Nearby was a stone-walled well, from which water was drawn in a bucket.

We continued along the side of the hill, passing several small cottages of cut stone with clay tile roofs, nestling among the coconut trees.

"Homes like these are replacing the huts of bamboo and thatch we built in the beginning," Radhakrishna said, stopping and bringing me up short behind him. At one cottage, a man and woman standing outside smiled shyly when they saw me.

Radhakrishna pointed out other landmarks: another pavil-ionlike building, where the villagers often gathered in their free time; a combined house and post office, from which the high-caste postmaster rushed out to discuss some village business with Radhakrishna; and, at the foot of the hill, a small quarry. "We're setting up a stonecutters' cooperative," Radhakrishna explained. "We hope someday it will employ most of the village."

We were soon climbing another hill, bare except for some grass and low scrub, with frequent rock outcroppings along the slope. "This hill is ours too, but we haven't done anything with it yet," Radhakrishna told me. "This is what the other land looked like in the beginning."

The contrast was amazing.

From where we stood we could see most of Danagram on the other two hills. The two hillsides were dotted with numerous small buildings. The tops of the hills were ringed by ridged ter-races built to catch rainfall and prevent erosion; the terraces were planted with young coconut trees and other cash crops. The bottom two-thirds of the hills were nearly covered by tall coconut palms and other growth.

Compared to the dusty villages I had seen across India, it looked like paradise.

◄ ►

And how had this seeming paradise come to occupy what had recently been barren wasteland? During my stay at Danagram, Radhakrishna provided the pieces of the story, which began in the mid-1940s.

"I was a recent university graduate, a prospective Communist, and involved in the movement for independence. Then, on a train trip across India, we made a stop near Gandhi's ashram at Sevagram. I decided to pay a visit there, out of curiosity—and to scoff.

"I wound up staying two years," he said.

For those two years, Radhakrishna was trained in Gandhian education and other aspects of constructive work. Then, immediately after Gandhi's death in 1948, Radhakrishna returned south with his wife, Nirmala, whom he had met at Sevagram, and several other constructive workers. They moved onto a small estate owned by Radhakrishna's family, in the small town of Ramnatkara, near the city of Calicut. There they opened a development center for Ramnatkara and surrounding villages.

In the beginning, the workers barely survived on private donations. "I used to go out during the day to find money for the evening meal," Radhakrishna told me.

Still they stuck to their work. They helped set up village industries, taught sanitation, did welfare work among Harijans, and began an elementary school based on Gandhian-style education. (This school was later expanded, and then converted to a Gandhian-style high school, at which Radhakrishna was still the principal.)

Then came the Gandhians' nationwide Bhoodan campaign. When Vinoba himself toured the area in 1957, a wealthy landowner donated almost 30 acres close to Ramnatkara, adjoining a smaller plot he had donated earlier.

"At that point I saw the possibility of a major experiment in community," Radhakrishna said. He arranged the donation of some additional adjoining land, bringing the total to about 50 acres. Nineteen Harijan families were settled on the land. Radhakrishna and his family themselves moved there in 1958, as soon as a residence could be built.

And that was the beginning of New Dawn Gift-Village.

"In the beginning, the Harijans looked on us as guardian angels," Radhakrishna said. "So it wasn't hard to convince them to declare this a Gramdan village."

Under the Gramdan arrangement, the families handed over the titles of their land to a village council. The families still kept

Navodaya Danagram

the use of their land, but yielded the rights to sell, lease, mortgage, and so on. This arrangement was informal; at the time of my visit, it had never yet been legalized. (Many Gandhian workers elsewhere had waited for enabling legislation from state governments before beginning to reorganize villages that had declared Gramdan. These delays had often proved fatal to their efforts.)

The village council was made up of all the men and the women of the village. Besides holding title to all village land, it handled all other affairs of the village, making decisions by consensus.

A village fund was set up, into which each family was expected to put one percent of its earnings. In addition, some of Danagram's land was set aside for common use.

So the village had organization—but not much else. Danagram's land was located on two (later three) steep, barren hills that were considered wasteland. "The donor thought this land was useless," Radhakrishna told me.

Led by the Gandhian workers, the villagers threw themselves into developing their bit of earth. They broke up the rock outcroppings with picks and removed them. They built earth terraces around the slopes so they could cultivate without losing the soil in heavy rains. They added organic matter to the soil. They planted many coconut trees, as well as cashew, banana, tapioca, and other cash crops.

The face of the hills began to change in other ways as well. The villagers dug wells for drinking water. They built community bath stalls and outhouses. They began two roads, to connect the village with the main road, two miles away. And they began to build themselves cottages of stone and tile.

All the work was done by the villagers themselves, working together, and using only the hand tools available to them. "We all learned the skills as we went along," Radhakrishna said.

At first all the work was volunteer. Radhakrishna supported much of the village on his salary from the school, while he and his family lived on the same economic level as the other villagers. Often it was hard even to buy enough to eat.

Later, foreign charities and government programs donated development funds, which the villagers used to buy materials and to pay themselves wages for their work.

Some of the government programs gave a village only partial funding for a project and required the village to make up the difference. Danagram was generally the only village in the area willing to meet this requirement, so it had no trouble getting accepted in these programs.

"In fact, we're a help to the local officials in meeting their quotas," Radhakrishna said. "But we're ready to badger them too, when they're slow to deliver help that's due us."

Hand in hand with Danagram's physical development went social development.

"In the beginning, we called everyone together often for village council meetings, to get them into the habit. They would quarrel sometimes, but they never let the quarrels get out of hand—because they knew that a hostile world outside was waiting to enslave them. Also, there was the reward of development resources if they could work together.

"You could say these meetings were an educational forum. Everyone learned how to deal with issues better, how to make better decisions. It helped them 'take possession' of the village, too, dealing with village business like that. Sometimes the issues weren't even important, but we brought them up to make everyone feel they were doing something—to build their self-confidence."

Over the years, the Gandhian workers also helped the Harijan villagers stand up to high-caste outsiders. "These people were often beaten," Radhakrishna said. "I began reporting the beatings to the police and getting the offenders to pay reparations." The beatings stopped, and the Harijans learned that they had rights after all.

"The adults here still show some subservience toward big people from outside the village. But the children have no such problems with anyone."

Through all this, the villagers came to see more and more the benefits of cooperation. Working together meant resources for development, pooling of talents and strengths, protection from injustice, and caring neighbors.

◄ ►

By the time of my visit, Danagram had grown—by buying more land and bringing in more families—until it covered about 100 acres and held about 50 families, totaling 350 people.

The economic hardships of Danagram's first years were mostly over. Foreign charities had increased their funding for development, and the cash crops on the village's common land also supplied funds.

"Now we're near a turning point," Radhakrishna told me. "Within a few years, the coconut trees on our common land will mature. The annual crop will earn enough to fund all Danagram's development needs. Then we won't be dependent on outside funds."

Individual families too enjoyed a greater measure of security. While garden vegetables improved their diet, coconut trees and other cash crops on their private plots supplemented their outside income. (Most of the village men worked outside the village as farmworkers or stonecutters.) Any villager in financial need could now get a temporary job from the village itself. Villagers could also borrow from the village fund on easy terms, or from banks on the guarantee of the village council—an important benefit, since, in India, credit on reasonable terms is normally out of reach for any but the affluent.

The village council now met less often and only set general policy, while village affairs were managed by an executive council chosen by consensus. (Radhakrishna was president of the village council and headed the executive council.)

An independent organization of village women—headed by Radhakrishna's wife, Nirmala—ran programs for women and small children. A youth group had charge of the village library and other village functions—an arrangement that helped to build leaders who could continue the development of the village.

Danagram was still expanding, by several ways.

"Families with land next to the village take part in most of our activities, but they're afraid at first to give up title to their land," Radhakrishna explained. "To them, the title represents security. Gradually, though, they're convinced they have greater security *in* the village—so they join.

"It's a slow process, but we're in no hurry."

The village also grew by buying bordering plots as they became available. The village council brought in landless families to settle on the newly-acquired land, selecting the families on the basis of need.

Most of the families who joined or were brought into the village were Harijan, while a few others were from low castes. "But some upper-caste families have joined too," Radhakrishna told me.

"Most of the upper-caste ones came for idealistic reasons—especially teachers from my school. Some others are children of landlords who formerly oppressed these very people, but who are now destitute themselves. Naturally, their coming to us for help gives our villagers a big ego boost."

Radhakrishna had his eye on some adjoining land on which the children of Danagram's original land donor had built their homes.

"It's good, flat land—much better than what we were given," Radhakrishna told me. Flashing his ferocious grin, he said, "I've told them I want their land. They are already involved in activities in the village or at the school. I will wait until the strategic moment, then apply just the right pressure, and draw those exploiters into the village."

Danagram also included one Muslim family; and Radhakrishna was luring a cluster of other Muslim families with the bait of a well, now being dug for them by the villagers.

To Radhakrishna, it was very important that Danagram be a mixed community. He was trying to show that Indians could live and work cooperatively, whatever their religion, caste, or lack of caste. In this way he would present an example to most Indian villages, plagued as they are by social division. Without diversity, he said, Danagram would have little relevance to the problems of those villages.

"We could declare this village a Harijan colony and become eligible for more government aid. But if we are only a Harijan colony, then this would all just be charity work.

"I'm not interested in that. It can't be revolutionary."

Of course, Danagram was still far from a typical Indian village. It was in fact an "intentional community"—a community started from scratch, with ground rules suited to the goals of its founders. The problems of creating unity here could not be as great as in a typical village, where divisions and unjust social structures had stood unchallenged for tens of generations.

Still, getting Indians from diverse social groups to live and work cooperatively was a significant achievement and important as a demonstration of what was possible. What's more, Danagram showed what villagers could accomplish when they pulled with, rather than against, each other—in that way showing the need of all Indian villages for such social unity.

◄ ►

The school bell rang, calling the students to change classes. About a dozen boys of junior high age rushed outdoors, grabbed short-handled digging forks, and began furiously loosening the earth in furrows where seeds would soon be planted. They grinned as they kept up a feverish pace. Meanwhile, a hundred yards away, Muslim girls in shawls stood in a line, passing water fire-bucket-style, to water banana plants twice the girls' height.

Such was the face of Gandhian education at Radhakrishna's school, Sevamandir ("Temple of Service").

The name Gandhi gave to the style of education developed in his ashrams was "basic education." The main idea behind it was to teach students how to produce life's basic necessities—food, clothing, and so on—while using this activity as a springboard to all other fields of knowledge.

For example, students kept records of their production, which required learning arithmetic; studying the design of craft equipment led them into geometry and mechanics; learning the development of a craft introduced history and geography. If a teacher was creative, any practical craft could be a window on the world.

Gandhi hoped that basic education would build citizens for the regenerated villages of his dreams.

It taught students skills that were needed in a self-reliant village economy, with techniques that improved on traditional

Students at Sevamandir

methods. By tying practical work to wider knowledge, basic education made this work come alive for the students, so that the work became a source of creativity instead of drudgery. And performing skilled handwork produced strong character, by building self-respect, a sense of responsibility, and a spirit of cooperation.

At the same time, Gandhi hoped to supplant the type of education introduced by the British. This schooling, aimed mainly at producing clerks for the colonial government bureaucracy, was creating an elite class that produced little of value, scorned Indian culture, and looked down on laboring Indians—while living off taxes paid from the fruit of that labor.

After India achieved independence, state and national governments made some gestures toward converting schools to basic education. But the effort was halfhearted and therefore short-lived.

India's education system today is not much different from what it was when inherited from the British.

Sevamandir, like nearly all other basic education schools around the country, was eventually pressured into adopting a standard curriculum. Radhakrishna, though, managed to salvage a bit of basic education—by adding it *on top of* that curriculum.

At Sevamandir, basic education primarily took the form of agriculture. Each of the school's 800 students spent one period a day caring for some of the school's acre of garden plots.

The plots, scattered among and around the school buildings, were sown with such crops as rice, beans, and tapioca. The produce was sold in the school's cooperative store (mostly to students and staff) and in the local market. The proceeds helped pay the school's operating costs.

Another aspect of basic education was that students helped run the school. The students at Sevamandir had their own government, with executive, legislative, and judicial branches.

The student judiciary handled most student discipline. The ministers in the executive branch planned and carried out programs in such areas as campus maintenance and sanitation, gardening, extracurricular activities, the library, the cooperative

store, health, student banking, and community service projects.
The legislature kept tabs on the ministers—and faculty members
too might at times be called on the carpet.

According to Radhakrishna, the advantages of this self-
government were many, for both students and teachers. Students developed confidence and self-respect by taking charge of
their own activities. They learned to be accountable to others,
while holding their leaders accountable to themselves. They
took pride in their school. There was a climate of self-discipline
and order; in fact, vandalism was almost unheard of at Sevamandir.

"At first the teachers were uneasy about so much responsibility being given to the students," Radhakrishna told me. "They
felt their own authority was being undermined, and they felt
threatened. But now they're completely won over by the advantages of a cooperative relationship."

The students too were apparently won over. "Many of them
come in on Saturdays and holidays to water the plants and to
work at other activities," said Radhakrishna. "They'd come on
Sunday too, if we would open the school for them."

Though Radhakrishna had for many years divided his time
and efforts between Danagram and Sevamandir, the two areas
of work were not for him essentially different. Danagram was
basically a form of social education, a way of teaching people to
live and work in harmony. And, in fact, he was teaching the
same at Sevamandir.

◄ ►

The future of any community depends on its children, and for
no community as much as for an intentional one such as
Danagram.

The eldest children of Danagram, having been educated at
Sevamandir, now attended a local college. In India, most college
graduates leave their villages far behind, usually taking government jobs and settling in urban centers.

Would Danagram's children do the same? Would they aban-
don Danagram, relegating it to the status of an interesting but
one-generational social experiment? Or would they stay to sus-
tain it as a true community?

This was a concern I expressed to Radhakrishna. On my final morning in the village, he brought it up to the young people attending a meeting of Danagram's executive council. Following a conversation in the local language, Radhakrishna translated for me.

"I asked them, 'What will it take to make you stay in the village?' They told me they need a communications infrastructure—which means the road must be finished—and they need enough investment capital to finance their ideas for developing the village.

"I told them that, if they stayed, I would take care of those things. So they agreed."

The young people looked on, beaming. Later in the morning, I overheard Radhakrishna telling them, "The village is in your hands."

In a way, Danagram was like one of Radhakrishna's coconut trees. He had sprouted the seed, planted it, stayed close to nurture it, and patiently tended its slow growth.

With such a dedicated, gifted cultivator, it was no wonder that the tree was bearing fruit.

7 *Five Villages and Four Hundred*

> My soul refuses to be satisfied so long as it is a helpless
> witness of a single wrong or a single misery.
>
> ◄ Gandhi

When I showed my photo of the hill tribesmen to Prem Bhai, head of the village development project called Agrindus Institute, his eyes took on a special glow. After a moment he said quietly, "You have really captured them."

I knew what he meant. The photo had caught the pride and strength that showed in the tribesmen's faces. In a way it was a tribute to Agrindus Institute. So many other development programs had sapped the initiative of their beneficiaries, leaving them in the role of helpless dependent.

Agrindus had created not dependents but partners. Instead of weakening their spirit, Agrindus was strengthening it.

That was one of the less tangible successes of Agrindus's program. The tangible successes had also been great. In fact, Agrindus was almost an anomaly in the field of village development—a project that set ambitious goals, actually met them, and sometimes even surpassed them. As such, it was in the forefront of the growing number of small- and middle-size nongovernment development projects spread across India.

Today there are several hundred of these projects, many run by

Tribesmen of the Agrindus Institute project area

Gandhians like Prem Bhai, others yet partly inspired by Gandhi's ideas. Such projects draw more and more attention as they prove more effective than large-scale government programs.

And among those drawing the most attention is Agrindus Institute.

Agrindus (short for "agroindustrial") is located near the southeastern tip of the central Indian state of Uttar Pradesh, in a hilly, forested region that holds 400 villages.

Most of the people living here are *adivasis*, a native tribal people found in many parts of India and making up about 7 percent of India's population. The adivasis descend from a people whose civilization was overrun during the conquest of India by Aryan tribes, almost 4,000 years ago. At that time, the ancestors of the adivasis fled into the hill forests, where their progeny have remained undisturbed until this century.

Now the modernization of India has encroached on the adivasis' homes. In the region served by Agrindus, natural resources have in the last few decades attracted industry, and industry has brought imported workers and a government presence. These in turn have meant crowding of the adivasis, harassment, and depletion of the forest.

The adivasis had always lived mostly on the wild produce of the forests; but with depletion of the forests, they were forced to take up farming. Because they had poor land and little farming skill, the adivasis suffered recurring famine.

It was during a severe famine in the mid-1960s that Prem Bhai first visited the region. (*Bhai* means "brother," a common form of address among Sarvodaya workers.) Having devoted thirteen years to study, observation, and experiment, Prem Bhai was ready to launch a major development project. He recognized this region as one of the most challenging in the country—so he decided to tackle it.

In 1967, building on an existing Gandhian facility, Prem Bhai and some fellow workers established Agrindus Institute.

◄ ►

My guide was an Agrindus worker named Rajendra Prasad, as I walked along narrow, hand-build dirt ridges bordering terraced fields on Agrindus's 150-acre model farm.

Young people at work among the crops smiled as we passed, and pointed me out to each other. We walked by a field of sugar cane, and Rajendra Prasad had a young man cut a stalk for me with a machete; then he showed me how to peel and chew it.

Rajendra Prasad showed me fields where rice and wheat were grown in succession; fields of vegetables, bananas, and cotton; orchards, in the distance. Scattered among the fields were artificial ponds and lakes—reservoirs that supplied water to the crops.

Yet, when Prem Bhai first came here, this land was exactly like most land in the area—hilly, stony, covered by forest and brush, and heavily eroded.

Prem Bhai

The development of this farm as a showplace and training center was the main work of Agrindus in its first few years. Prem Bhai hired adivasi villagers to clear and shape the land, which in itself helped train the villagers in land reclamation.

With a combination of land shaping and modern farming methods, Prem Bhai was soon raising *five to ten times more* per acre than the local farmers.

The key to this success was the reservoirs. As Prem Bhai explained, the major cause of crop failure in this region was drought. But drought in India was not usually a lack of rain—it was rain falling at the wrong time.

Like most of India, this region had almost all its rainfall in several months of monsoon beginning in late summer. Normally this was the only water that fields received during the year—so crops had to be planted at just the right time to benefit from it. If the monsoon rains came too late, or came and ended too early, crops withered and died. The problem, then, was to collect the monsoon rains for controlled use—which was what the reservoirs did.

Each reservoir was formed by building an earth wall across the mouth of a small valley. The reservoir collected water during the monsoons; then the water slowly seeped through the earth dam to irrigate the field beyond it. In some cases, water from the reservoir was also pumped to fields at a higher level.

An earth-dam reservoir does have one drawback, as a Gandhian agricultural expert cautioned me. The rate of seepage can't be controlled, so that often more water is supplied than is needed. A field drainage system therefore must be added soon, or else the excess of water can render the field salty and useless within a decade—a danger that Agrindus had not yet addressed.

But, given this precaution, the earth-dam method was especially suited to poor, remote villages like those in the Agrindus area. The reservoirs could be built with nothing more than hand labor and simple tools, by the adivasis themselves. In most cases, irrigation from the reservoirs used the force of gravity alone, so no outside energy source was needed.

For such reservoirs, the villagers did not have to wait for a distant bureaucracy to organize an expensive, complex project—as they would have if the government built a major dam and irrigation system. Also unlike government projects, these small reservoirs did not displace dozens or hundreds of villages.

Prem Bhai figured that this irrigation method alone could provide water for almost three-quarters of the area's farmland.

Besides protecting against drought, the reservoirs enabled Prem Bhai to depart from local farming practices in other ways. The reservoirs provided enough water to grow crops most of the year, meaning two or three crops in a row, instead of the usual one (or none). The usual main crop of millet could be replaced by rice and wheat, which gave higher yields and were more nutritious.

Besides that, the rice and wheat could be raised from hybrid seed (requiring more water), which yielded still more. Also used were chemical fertilizer and pesticide—especially required by these hybrid seeds—supplemented by organic fertilizers such as compost and manure.

Aside from the partial use of organic fertilizer, there was little that was novel in these methods. Irrigation, hybrid seed, chemical fertilizer, and pesticide were the essential ingredients of the "Green Revolution"—a campaign begun by government and private development agencies in the early 1960s to modernize Third World agriculture.

The Green Revolution had dramatically increased the grain harvests in many countries, including India. The farmers who had benefited, though, were mostly the richer ones, with the education, capital, and acreage to adopt the new technology profitably.

The achievement of Agrindus and similar development projects was to bring the Green Revolution to the village poor.

But perhaps this was a mixed blessing.

At a time when Western-style "chemical farming" is more and more questioned in the West itself, it may be doubtful wisdom to introduce it into Indian villages—even with the moderating use of organic fertilizer. (Gandhi himself spoke out against chemical methods, and praised the budding movement for organic agriculture.)

The yield of crops grown in this region could have been greatly increased by irrigation alone, without hybrid seed, chemical fertilizer, or pesticide. The increase probably wouldn't have been as quick or as steep. But a slower rate of progress might have been justified, if that was the cost of establishing farming practices that were more healthful, more self-reliant, and more beneficial to the land in the long run.

Or did the human suffering at hand overturn such considerations?

◄ ►

The Agrindus center included facilities for other parts of Agrindus's development program as well.

At the Agrindus dairy, Western and Indian strains of cattle were being cross-bred. Nearby, a small methane gas plant converted cowdung into gas fuel for the Agrindus kitchen, as well as into fertilizer.

A junior high school boarded about 80 village children. The children attended classes in the morning, then worked in the fields in the afternoon, both as training and in order to grow the crops that fed them and paid their school expenses. Young people past junior high age were being trained for a wide variety of occupations—civil engineer, dairy manager, mechanic, blacksmith, electrician, village administrator, development worker.

A clinic dispensed medical care at nominal rates to the villagers as it served as a training ground for young people preparing there to serve their villages as doctors and paramedics. The clinic was directed by Dr. Ragini Prem, Prem Bhai's wife, a handsome, thoughtful woman who headed Agrindus's health and family welfare program.

Another part of Dr. Prem's program was educational outreach to the villages on basic health practices, such as nutrition, sanitation, and first aid—practices that were helping to stem the area's high rate of epidemics. Her program also promoted family planning (birth control).

The family planning part of the program had at first met with great resistance from the adivasis. As Dr. Prem herself pointed out, most poor people throughout the world *want* large families, because they see children as extra workers to help feed the family and as a support in their coming old age. With a high child death rate, the only way to make sure that any children survive is to have many of them. This attitude is not likely to change unless health and economic conditions improve.

But Agrindus's other programs were now providing the improved conditions in area villages, and birth control was starting to catch on.

"The villagers are much more in favor of a small family now," Dr. Prem told me. But she added, "The upcoming generation

Dr. Ragini Prem

will show whether family planning is catching on. The older generation hasn't much hope of it."

To Dr. Prem, family planning was not just a way to curb population growth.

"Family planning is needed whether one wants a large or a small family, whether the population is growing or shrinking," she said. "It is not only a way to stop having children but a way to decide when to have children, and how many. It gives families some control over their lives."

◄ ►

The first Agrindus worker to settle in the surrounding villages was Rama Shanker Bhai. His initiative led to the program that became the showcase of the Agrindus method.

Rama Shanker Bhai had already been a Sarvodaya worker before coming to Agrindus. Between 1967 and 1970 he stayed at

Rama Shanker Bhai

the Agrindus center to be trained in Agrindus's farming methods. Then, in 1971, he left the center to settle in Bakulia, one of five villages in an area two hours' drive away, over rough dirt roads and through a forest. "I took two sets of clothes, and went to live in the house of a friend," he told me.

He spent the next year talking with the villagers, learning about their problems—which were many and severe:

Almost all the 1,500 residents of the five villages went hungry much of the time, and most *never* had enough to eat.

Poor weather caused a crop failure almost every other year, while livestock often died of hunger and thirst. Even when the weather was right, a third of the land might lie idle, because plow animals had died, or because farmers could not afford seed. And farmers couldn't find employment to bring in extra money.

The adivasis also suffered harassment by outsiders. Police and government workers of all types abused them.

"These people from outside used to come and force the villagers to work for no pay," Rama Shanker Bhai said. "Or they would take goats and chickens from their houses. They would beat the villagers to make them do what they wanted. Or, if they had come alone, they would get their way by making vague threats."

Often the outsiders wanted bribes. The police would come and threaten to arrest villagers on false charges if the officers weren't paid off. Tax collectors demanded bribes to record tax payments villagers made to them. A government vaccinator took bribes not to inject the villagers in the wrong spot. The adivasis had taken to running into the forest whenever they saw a neatly dressed person.

But the villagers' main problem, it turned out, was moneylenders.

These moneylenders were mostly non-adivasi villagers from the plains, who had been displaced into the hills when a government-built dam made a reservoir of their valley. The adivasi villagers, who had no previous experience of moneylenders, were soon deeply in debt.

Most of the families owed more than a villager's normal yearly earnings. The moneylenders charged between 25 and 200 percent interest, so the families could never hope to pay off the debt from their own resources.

Often a moneylender would take a farmer's entire crop just for an interest payment. At other times he might take a member of the family as a "bonded laborer," in a form of semi-slavery that could even be passed from one generation to the next. (Both bonded labor and moneylending at outrageous rates are the norm in India's villages.)

"The villagers couldn't read," Rama Shanker Bhai said, "so the moneylenders would cheat them by falsifying the records of the debt. They could do anything they liked. If a villager wouldn't pay, the moneylender would come and have him beaten up and just take the money."

To cap all their other problems, the village men had taken to drinking heavily.

Rama Shanker Bhai decided to try to deal with the moneylender problem.

"I told the villagers, 'If you want to get free of the moneylenders, form a village fund, and then you won't have to borrow from them.' " So a village fund and a village council were organized in each village. The villagers also donated land and labor to build a cottage to serve as an Agrindus outpost and home for Rama Shanker Bhai.

The moneylenders didn't like what Rama Shanker Bhai was doing. "They tried to talk the villagers out of going along with me," Rama Shanker Bhai said, "but nobody listened to them.

"One moneylender even came and threatened to shoot me. I told him, 'Go ahead and shoot. I'm not afraid of you.' They might have killed me, if the Agrindus center hadn't been close by."

Threatened though the moneylenders may have felt, Rama Shanker Bhai made little headway against them. The reason was simple: The villagers needed credit, and, despite the establishment of a village fund, the moneylenders were yet the only adequate source. The villagers could not get free of the moneylenders without somehow first improving their financial situation.

Rama Shanker Bhai saw he needed a more comprehensive approach.

He made a detailed survey of village conditions; then he and the Agrindus central staff worked out a three-year program. The plan emphasized farming improvements, which Agrindus believed had to be the basis of any village economic development.

To implement the plan, Agrindus supplied training and other support services, while the actual work was organized by the village councils, under Rama Shanker Bhai's guidance. The plan was financed with money raised by Agrindus but administered by the village councils. The councils disbursed this money to village families through revolving loan funds, with the neediest families receiving loans first.

The plan worked like this: Say that a family had been slated for improvements on its land. These improvements might include leveling and terracing, or constructing a small reservoir for irrigation.

The village council would then loan the family enough money to hire a number of other villagers to work on the projects. In this way, the Agrindus plan provided not only improvements but also paid jobs—in fact, enough to employ every villager who needed work.

This loan for major projects would be supplemented by loans for seed, fertilizer, pesticide, a plow animal—anything Agrindus figured the family needed for a successful crop. At the same time, the farmer would receive agricultural training from Agrindus workers, right in the village fields.

The normal result was that the family's land would immediately start producing many times more than it had before. Most families, therefore, could pay back their loans to the village council within a year, making the money available to other families.

In this way, a limited fund could help all the families in the five villages within three years. What's more, when the plan period ended, the money was still there, ready for further use.

Over three years, about 7 percent of the villages' farmland was leveled and shaped. More than double that amount was irrigated through almost 100 small-scale projects. All the families were supplied seed, fertilizer, and pesticide; and plow animals were furnished where needed.

For the five villages as a whole, the crop yield more than doubled.

Families with less land were helped in other ways. About a third of the village families were supplied dairy animals—cows, buffalo, or goats—while several other families were helped to set up small village industries.

At the end of the plan's three years, the villagers were still poor—but the extremes of poverty had been eliminated.

Now the villagers were carrying out a second-phase program, continuing with farm improvements, but with an added focus on village industries. Agrindus expected this plan to lift all the families of the five villages out of poverty within five years.

◄ ►

Besides generally improving the villagers' financial condition, the five villages development program had provided Rama Shanker Bhai ammunition in his continuing fight against the moneylenders—a fight that was vital, if the villagers were to hold onto their gains. Because of the program, there was much less need to borrow from the moneylenders. The villagers had more cash and had the revolving loan fund as a source of credit for annual farming needs (seed and so on).

Rama Shanker Bhai further cut down this need for borrowing by leading some of the villagers in a campaign against two other major causes for villagers going into debt: expensive weddings and the practice of dowry.

"First we tried to talk the young people out of it during literacy classes. Then I started going with a group of the villagers to weddings, to preach against dowry. We also pushed for fewer musicians at the weddings, since these are so expensive."

Within two or three years, these costly practices had been dropped.

During this time, Rama Shanker Bhai also led his village brigade in a campaign against drinking.

"We told them, 'Your economic condition suffers, you misbehave with the women, you start fighting, and the women leave you because of it.' Some were converted by this. Then we started visiting homes to find out who was still drinking and to talk to them about it.

"We also picketed the local shops. After a few months, their licenses were revoked.

"Now only a fraction of the villagers drink—and that is on the sly. When we hear that someone has been making contraband liquor, we go to their house and say, 'Will you own up, or do we search?' Usually they bring out the equipment, and then we bust it up."

All these measures helped in the fight against the moneylenders. But they were not enough—because payments on existing debts alone would have wiped out any economic gains the villagers made.

So Rama Shanker Bhai had to tackle the moneylenders directly as well.

"I would go with a number of villagers to see the moneylender, and we'd ask to see the record of a debt. I'd tell him, 'If the record is truthful, we will pay it. But if you show us a false record, or none at all, you'll get nothing.'

"When he showed us the record, we would check it right there with the one who owed the debt. If it was all right, we repaid the loan on the spot." The money would come from the revolving loan fund, which the borrower would then reimburse in easy installments.

In this way, all debts to outsiders had been settled, and all bonded laborers had been freed. No villager had yet fallen back into debt.

The power of the moneylenders had been broken.

Rama Shanker Bhai had also set an example to the villagers on how to deal with other outsiders.

"The police always go around and ask if there have been any fights. In one of our villages, they heard about a fight between a husband and a wife. They told the couple they were going to jail!

"I said to them, 'Do you have a warrant?' They said, 'No.' I said, 'Then you can't take them.' They were looking for a bribe not to arrest these two. If there are no problems in the village, the police are out of work.

"The forest rangers live in the village, so they are even worse than the police. The law lets people take a few pieces of wood from the forest, but the rangers always threaten them.

"One villager cut a wood pole for a well. The ranger demanded a bribe not to start a court case against him. The villager paid, but he came and told me. So I went to the ranger and demanded a receipt or the return of the money.

"The ranger said, 'I can't give a receipt, because I wasn't supposed to take the money. But I can't give the money back, because it would disgrace me. Here, you take the money and keep it for yourself.'

"But I wouldn't take it. Finally, he returned the money to the villager. He said to me, 'Next time tell me if it's one of your men so I won't ask for money.' "

The villagers began to follow Rama Shanker Bhai's example.

"One time a tax collector left his bicycle in the house of one of the villagers. A village boy used it once, and something went wrong with it. The tax collector demanded 200 rupees, the cost of the bike. The villagers said, 'All right, but we will keep the bike.' The tax collector said, 'No.' He wanted the money *and* the bike.

"He started beating the boy. So the villagers started beating *him*. Then they tied him to a cot and carried him to the center.

"When they got there, the Agrindus people said, 'Why did you carry him? Why didn't you make him walk?' "

Now all visitors to the villages had to fill out a form stating the purpose of their visit, and sign it, before the villagers would deal with them. When villagers went themselves to visit government officials, they went in groups, so they could not be so easily intimidated. And a "people's committee," composed mostly of young people, had been formed in each village to deal with abuses by outsiders.

◀ ▶

The story of the five villages points up some basic principles of the Agrindus approach.

One is that the villagers themselves must take an active role in development—because the main goal of development is not to give aid to the villagers but to organize and inspire them to help themselves.

Though some amount of outside aid is usually needed, villagers need to make a matching effort, or the aid will only breed dependence and greater helplessness. Village development efforts in India have often left the villagers waiting placidly for more handouts.

An active role for the villagers also helps ensure that planning meets their real needs, rather than the needs imagined for them by a distant bureaucrat.

A second principle is that development should focus on the community as a whole. An entire village working together can achieve much more than any individual or small group.

What's more, programs that focus on individuals or groups usually end up widening the gap between rich and poor— because the rich are generally the ones best able to take advantage of them.

This has been the fate of almost all government development efforts in India. Even where development programs reach the poor, if the benefits are not spread evenly within the community, the programs often create division, tension, and conflict.

A third principle is that the development of the village must be tackled from many angles at once—economic, social, political, and so on—because all these aspects are related.

In the five villages, this was reflected in the fact that the moneylenders could not be effectively dealt with until the villagers' financial condition had improved—yet their financial condition could not be much improved until the moneylenders were dealt with.

Piecemeal development programs often fall flat because planners ignore seemingly unrelated facts of village life.

A fourth principle is that the development process benefits from what Agrindus calls a "continuum" of development workers. It takes an organization of fair size to gather resources for village development—funds, training facilities, equipment, expertise, and so on. But effective development also requires day-to-day contact with the villagers, best done by workers living among the villagers themselves.

Agrindus's combination of central institute with village-based worker was one of the main reasons for its success in delivering development to the villages.

Finally, the story of the five villages emphasizes the importance of the qualifications of that village worker. No matter how well structured a development program is, or how much money is put into it, its results still depend on the quality of that individual—and on his or her commitment to stick with the community for the long haul.

The outstanding success of the five villages program was largely due to an outstanding, committed worker: Rama Shanker Bhai.

◄ ►

At the same time that the five villages plan was implemented, another plan was launched for 100 villages.

This plan worked much the same way as the five villages program did, except that money was available to fewer families in a village at a time. Agrindus acted as a center of operations—coordinating plans, raising funds, training villagers, and so on. Subcenters, each staffed by several workers, operated within groups of 15 to 25 villages.

Parallel to the Agrindus structure was a hierarchy of organizations run by villagers, at the village, subcenter, and program area levels.

With Agrindus's guidance, these village organizations had the major role in devising and carrying out plans. They also decided how all project funds should be allocated, with Agrindus itself acting only as treasurer—disbursing funds as directed, keeping records, and so on.

For this administrative work and its other services, Agrindus imposed a 5 percent service charge on loans, which paid Agrindus staff salaries and other program expenses.

At the time of my visit, the 100-village plan had been extended for an indefinite period and expanded to cover almost 150 villages; and Agrindus hoped to include all 400 villages of its project area, within several more years. Problems had arisen in some plan villages, though, due to tensions possibly caused by Agrindus workers pushing economic development ahead of village unity.

Also at this time, Agrindus was seeking funds for a new program aimed at developing village industries in the 400 villages.

The program would use many of the elements that had proved successful in Agrindus's existing village development programs, including loans from a revolving fund.

The program would create many small production units, using equipment based on small-scale, "intermediate technology." The units would draw most of their raw materials from local resources and also sell most of their products locally. Proposed industries included textiles, rope-making, beekeeping, forest produce, basic food processing (flour-grinding and the like), lime-quarrying, brick-making, carpentry, and farm tools manufacturing.

At the moment, the area's village industry was in decline. Yet, if the resources at hand were put to use, Prem Bhai believed, they would create enough work for all the villagers now forced into idleness.

Agrindus also had ambitious plans concerning the financing of its programs.

Because most of Agrindus's programs issued loans instead of grants, Agrindus's development funds didn't get used up—they only grew, as more funds were raised from the government and from charities. So, within five to ten years, Agrindus might have collected all the funds it would ever need. Agrindus's own operating expenses would then be covered by the 5 percent service charge it imposed on loans. And if extra money *were* needed for a large project, existing assets would make it possible to qualify for large bank loans.

Once Agrindus's funding was secure, Prem Bhai told me, the fight against local injustices might become more aggressive.

"For instance, we might lead the villagers in nonviolent actions against the government, to force it to provide basic services the villages are supposed to receive, or to stop it from allowing forest resources to be taken out too fast. We can do this when we are strong. But first the villages must free themselves of their own social faults.

"Eventually, I would like to see the village governments take over the local functions of the state and national governments—though this might not happen in my lifetime. Centralization of society leaves you open to breakdowns of the system, to outside control of your basic needs, to blackmail, sabotage, and so on. Self-sufficiency makes you independent."

Might there be a time when Agrindus itself was no longer needed?

Prem Bhai smiled. "It would be a great thing if they threw me out."

◄ ►

Prem Bhai believed that Agrindus's basic approach could work anywhere else in India. Yet Agrindus and other Gandhian development projects now affect mainly the outskirts of Indian society—adivasis, Harijan colonies, small mountain villages, and the like. Those villages are already more unified than most, with the villagers more willing to work together.

The Gandhians have not yet dealt effectively with typical Indian villages and their severe social and economic divisions.

Still, this uplift of marginal and oppressed groups is itself a valuable goal; and such weak groups make up a large portion of India's people. It may turn out that the greatest accomplishment of the Sarvodaya Movement will have been its efforts in this field.

Despite the much greater ambitions of many of the Gandhians, this by itself would be a great contribution.

8 Postscript: Other Lands

If I can say so without arrogance and with due humility, my
message and methods are indeed, in their essentials, for the
whole world.

◂ Gandhi

Jai jagat!—*Victory to the world!*

◂ Vinoba

No look at Gandhi's successors would be complete without at
least a glance at some of the people and groups around the world
who have been strongly influenced by him.

◂ ▸

Among these are a number of United States organizations. The
largest are the Fellowship of Reconciliation, made up of religious
pacifists; and the War Resisters League, with a generally more
secular, leftist membership.

These and allied organizations have been at or near the center
of all the major nonviolent action movements that have shaken
United States society since World War II: the disarmament
movement of the late 1950s and early 1960s; the civil rights
movement (supporting Martin Luther King, Jr., and the
Southern Christian Leadership Conference); the antiwar movement of the '60s; the movement against nuclear power in the
'70s; and the resurgent disarmament movement of the '80s.

A relative newcomer among these organizations, but an influential one, is Movement for a New Society. Founded in 1971 mostly by Quakers, MNS is a nationwide network of nonviolent activists, with its most important center of activity in Philadelphia. Antinuclear groups and others across the United States today use training techniques and business meeting formats disseminated by MNS.

Though the membership of the mentioned organizations is mostly white, two of the most dramatic examples of nonviolent action in the United States have been movements by racial minorities. One, of course, was the civil rights movement led mainly by Martin Luther King, Jr., who was directly inspired by his study of Gandhi. The other is the effort led by Cesar Chavez to organize a union for Chicano and Filipino farmworkers in California.

Chavez's United Farm Workers of America (UFW) has been built in the face of fierce opposition by California growers. The union has confronted this opposition with strikes and with calls for nationwide consumer and retailer boycotts of certain wines, table grapes, and lettuce. In 1975, at the height of the boycotts, 12 percent of United States adults surveyed in a Gallup Poll said they were boycotting California table grapes.

The UFW campaigns resulted in a California law that establishes the right of farm workers to belong to a union. The campaigns also raised wages from under $1 an hour in the early 1960s, to as high as $5; won elementary benefits; and made important improvements in hiring practices and living and working conditions, including some protection from pesticides.

Grower opposition, though, remains fierce and effective, so union efforts continue as well. In 1984, the union launched a new international boycott of California table grapes.

◄ ►

Not only Gandhi's action techniques but also his social vision has inspired American efforts. A prime example is the community land trust movement, launched in the late '60s by maverick economist Ralph Borsodi and nonviolent activist Robert Swann as a United States version of Gramdan.

A community land trust is an organization that acquires land and holds it "in trust" for the entire community.

Governing trustees include the land users, members of the surrounding community, and technical experts, all making decisions together by consensus or near-consensus. The land itself is leased to its users on an indefinite, protected basis, but with restrictions on what the land may be used for and on practices that would harm the land.

As Bob Swann explains, this arrangement has a number of advantages over normal private ownership. For instance, it keeps land available to those who aren't wealthy, by preventing its sale to large landowners and real estate speculators. A number of land trusts have been set up specially to provide land to the very poor who could never afford it otherwise.

The land trust arrangement also can make sure that land is used in ways that best benefit the community—for example, by protecting prime farmland from urban sprawl. And it can prevent damage to the land from such practices as strip-mining or clear-cutting of forests.

An advantage of the land trust arrangement over conventional socialism is that control of the land remains local, shared by the community and the land users themselves—all of those most affected by how the land is used.

By 1980, there were 35 to 40 community land trusts nationwide, based more or less on the original model. Most were rural, though others were "urban land trusts," mostly concerned with housing.

Bob Swann is also seeking to apply the concept to industry. Trustees of an "industrial trust" would include workers, managers, technical experts, and members of the larger community. The industrial trust, Swann says, is a step beyond the concept of either the consumer or the worker co-op, as it merges the main features of each.

◄ ►

Many Britons have learned lessons from that country's former Indian adversary, and many of the United States organizations influenced by Gandhi have their counterparts in Britain. Their activity can be seen in the "peace camps" that have sprung up around military bases in the 1980s and in other actions in the movement against nuclear weapons.

Britain is also home base for the Intermediate Technology Development Group, one of a number of organizations carrying forward Gandhi's idea of technology aimed at village needs. ITDG's principal founder was the late E. F. Schumacher—best known for his book *Small Is Beautiful*—whose background included serious study of Gandhian economics, as well as close contact with the Gandhians in India.

Founded in 1965, ITDG is now the central point in a network of affiliate organizations in developed and developing countries alike. These centers search out "appropriate technology" that already exists, develop new technology to fill gaps, and make available the total to development workers and community organizers around the world. Areas of research include buildings, clothes, farm tools, water, power, and health.

◀ ▶

Across the English Channel, in the mountains of southern France, lies the Community of the Ark, founded by the man often called "Gandhi's first disciple in the West," the late Lanza del Vasto. Begun in 1948, it now occupies 1,200 acres of farmland and forest, with over 100 permanent and temporary residents of all ages and many nations.

The Ark is an attempt to build a model society based on the Gandhian and Christian principles of nonviolence and simplicity, as interpreted by its founder. Community members farm, raise dairy animals, spin, weave, and practice other crafts, trying to be self-sufficient, and using almost no electricity or motorized equipment.

They govern themselves primarily by consensus; and they use no methods of group discipline other than sacrificial acts by individuals appealing to the conscience of another. Joyful celebration, song, and devotion to beauty are important elements of community life.

Lanza del Vasto and his followers were among the first to introduce Gandhian nonviolent action to France and to Catho-

The Common Room, the Community of the Ark

lics worldwide. Many of their actions were directed against French militarism in the period of the French–Algerian War (1954–1962)—the French equivalent of the United States war in Vietnam.

More recently, the Ark helped farmers of the neighboring Larzac plateau launch a campaign to halt expropriation of their lands for the expansion of an army base. With a series of creative nonviolent actions, the farmers and their many supporters stalled the expansion from 1970 to 1981, when the newly elected Socialist government bowed to popular sentiment and canceled the project.

In the early '70s, the Larzac campaign helped inspire the birth of the European anti-nuclear-power movement. This in turn directly inspired the American Seabrook campaign, prototype for most of the later United States nuclear power plant "occupations."

The Ark now has a number of branch communities in France, Spain, Italy, and Quebec, as well as an international network of "Friends of the Ark." By promoting the founding of nonviolent, self-sufficient communities, it would like to create centers from which Western civilization can be rebuilt after collapse—a collapse it sees as inevitable, from one cause or another.

◀ ▶

"The Gandhi of Sicily" is the name often given to Danilo Dolci.

Dolci arrived in Sicily—a semiautonomous island off the tip of Italy—in 1952, to live among its poverty-stricken people and help them improve their lot. In the following years, he led a number of campaigns pressuring the Italian government to deliver on promises of aid to the region. Among the creative techniques he and his followers used were a mass fast and a "strike-in-reverse"—1,200 unemployed Sicilians repairing a road that local officials had neglected. (Both actions drew physical abuse from police.)

Dolci has set up a number of centers throughout western Sicily that work to organize cooperatives and unions and in other ways to improve village life.

He has also actively opposed the Mafia, including exposing government officials with Mafia ties and organizing local action groups. Dolci's theory is that the Mafia can thrive only where people distrust each other and keep to themselves; so his main strategy has been to encourage cooperative efforts that unite communities. The Mafia has been noticeably weaker in areas where he and his colleagues have worked.

More recently, Dolci has given most of his attention to a school founded by him, which attempts to present an alternative form of education for Italy. Like Gandhi with his "basic education," Dolci sees the proper nurturing of children as vital in building a new society.

◄ ►

In Sri Lanka—an island nation off the southern tip of India—leaders of the minority Tamil race have used Gandhian nonviolent action since 1956 to protest discrimination by the dominant Sinhalese.

Most of the action has taken place in the northeast corner of the island, where Tamils form a majority. Tactics there have included general strikes, fasting, blockades of government offices, and the illegal setting up of an alternative postal service.

In 1976, having received no satisfaction from the government, the activists formed the Tamil United Liberation Front to press for a separate Tamil nation. TULF, committed to Gandhian nonviolence, is the major established political voice of the Tamil people. Its efforts, though, are now overshadowed by those of Tamil guerrillas, who have helped lead the country steadily down the path of civil war.

Also on Sri Lanka, mostly among the Sinhalese, is another Gandhian-inspired group, called the Sarvodaya Shramadana Movement—"Movement for the Awakening of All, Through the Gift of Work."

Sarvodaya Shramadana aims at village development throughout Sri Lanka, drawing on the example of Gramdan for much of its method, but basing its philosophy on principles of Buddhism, the major faith among the Sinhalese. The movement's activities have touched over 2,000 of Sri Lanka's 17,000 villages, and it now receives strong support from the government and from international agencies. Like the Indian movement, though, Sarvodaya Shramadana seems to have spread its efforts too thin.

◄ ►

Over the past two and a half decades, the Unified Buddhist Church of South Vietnam has conducted campaigns inspired by Gandhi and Martin Luther King, Jr.

In 1963, Buddhist monks (men and women) led a mass campaign against the United States–backed Diem regime, for its denial of religious freedom to Buddhists. (South Vietnam is 85 percent Buddhist.)

Alongside more conventional methods of protest, the monks introduced what to many was a shocking innovation in nonviolent technique: self-immolation. Individual monks doused themselves with gasoline, then lit matches to themselves. Though this form of protest baffled and repelled many, it was a self-sacrifice that brought attention to the monks' cause from an electrified world.

The countrywide campaign destroyed Diem's base of support and culminated in a swift, nearly bloodless coup led by a general who was sympathetic to the popular cause. Shortly after, though, the government passed into the hands of military men determined to carry on the war. The Buddhists then redirected their movement toward ending fighting by both sides.

In 1966, the Buddhists' campaign to overthrow the Ky government was halted only by United States intervention.

In 1974, following official declaration of a ceasefire, the Buddhists launched a campaign to have it honored, encouraging South Vietnamese soldiers to refuse to fight. This was a major reason why in 1975 the South Vietnamese army seemed to "dissolve" in the face of the guerrillas' final offensive—an outcome not intended by the Buddhists, but welcomed by them as finally bringing an end to the war.

Following reunification of the country, the Buddhists declared their readiness to help in national reconstruction and reconciliation efforts. But the new Marxist rulers were no better disposed to the monks than the former rulers had been. They denied independent status to the Unified Buddhist Church, shut down most of the extensive social services run by it, and threw its top leaders into prison.

The monks resumed their resistance—including self-immolations. But government censorship of news has prevented a strong public response in their support.

◄ ►

International organizations too have been influenced by Gandhi. The Fellowship of Reconciliation and the War Resisters

League in the United States have their world counterparts in the International Fellowship of Reconciliation and War Resisters International, each with chapters and affiliates in many countries.

Another such organization is Nonviolent Alternatives, a world network founded in 1977 on the inspiration of Archbishop Dom Helder Camara of Brazil. In Latin America itself, nonviolent social change efforts are supported and linked by Servicio Paz y Justicia—"Service for Peace and Justice"—headed by Nobel Peace Prize winner Adolfo Perez Esquivel.

While *activists* are linked by the above organizations, a network has also grown up among peace *researchers*. The field of peace research has developed mostly since World War II, applying the methods of social science to such subjects as conflict resolution, national and international security systems, issues of social justice, and nonviolent action.

One of the more important areas of research has been the Gandhian idea of nonviolent civilian defense (also called "social defense," or "civilian-based defense")—using nonviolent action to resist foreign invasion. Pioneers in this field include Gene Sharp in the United States; April Carter, Theodor Ebert, and Adam Roberts in England; and Arne Naess and Johan Galtung in Norway.

Using scattered historical examples and practical analysis, these researchers have been working to develop strategies that could be adopted by governments in place of conventional military defense. Several Scandinavian countries have in part adopted the concept by initiating training programs for civilians.

Nonviolent civilian defense is one alternative to international violence; another is "peace brigades," as embodied in India's Shanti Sena, the World Peace Brigade, and subsequent international projects. As reported in chapter 3, this concept has seen a strong revival over the last few years, in such forms as Peace Brigades International.

As of 1986, the largest of any peace brigade effort is taking place under the name Witness for Peace—a campaign of United States Christians to oppose U.S.-backed guerrilla warfare in Nicaragua, as well as potential direct U.S. involvement.

Since 1983, Witness for Peace has sent more than 2,000 Americans to Nicaragua for terms of two weeks or six months. These people hold vigils in danger zones, document rebel activity, and do manual work alongside villagers. On their return to the United States, they take part in public education and political action. Many others who do not go to Nicaragua help with local support work.

◄ ►

Finally, 1986 saw one of history's most impressive examples of nonviolent action, in the February overthrow of Philippine President Ferdinand Marcos.

Marcos's removal capped a series of events starting with the 1983 assassination of opposition leader Benigno Aquino, who had hoped to apply his study of Gandhi to the Philippine situation. Following this, his wife, Corazon Aquino, became the rallying point for opposition efforts and the chief 1985 presidential candidate opposing Marcos.

Though Marcos claimed victory, the election was so marked by fraud and violence that his claim was widely rejected in the Philippines and abroad. To challenge Marcos's right to office, Aquino and her associates planned a popular campaign of general strikes, government boycotts, and civil disobedience, which they expected to last many months. But the campaign was preempted in February by the revolt and defection to the Aquino cause of two top military leaders and a few hundred troops, who barricaded themselves in a Manila military camp.

An urgent radio appeal by a Catholic church leader and an Aquino associate brought hundreds of thousands of men, women, and children into the streets of Manila to nonviolently support and defend the rebelling troops. Though the limited military revolt itself posed no serious threat to Marcos, his armed forces were hindered from defeating or even attacking the rebels by the peaceful interposition of the civilians; and the civilians' friendly appeals led to further troop defections and widespread ignoring of orders.

Marcos, faced with this popular resistance, this loss of control over his armed forces, and the withdrawal of crucial support from the United States government, fled the country.

The nonviolent nature of Marcos's overthrow was no accident or coincidence. Aside from the Gandhian background of Benigno Aquino, church and opposition leaders and others had been prepared by years of discussion and training in nonviolent methods. For instance, International Fellowship of Reconciliation officials in 1984 and 1985 led dozens of nonviolent action workshops for hundreds of clergy and lay people, including Aquino family members. Such workshops continued to be held by AKKAPKA, a new Philippine IFOR chapter, up through the events of February.

◄ ►

These are just a few of today's people, groups, and movements influenced by Gandhi. Many more could be added:

◄ A "peace navy" in New Zealand blocking port entry of nuclear-armed warships and submarines.

◄ An adviser to Lech Walesa, leader of Poland's Solidarity movement, at the height of that movement.

◄ Native people of Norway blocking construction of a dam that would flood their homeland.

◄ A movement mostly of women trying to reconcile Protestants and Catholics in northern Ireland.

◄ American Indians establishing a camp in the Black Hills of South Dakota on land illegally taken from their ancestors by the United States government.

◄ A peace center in Jerusalem reconciling Jews and Arabs, while offering nonviolent action as an alternative to violence.

In ever-widening circles, Gandhi's legacy has been spreading through the consciousness of the world. As more and more people become ready to hear his message, it will continue to reach out, to new peoples, new generations.

It will be adapted to the time and place, sometimes improved, sometimes compromised. But it will not disappear.

It cannot. Because the spirit of the warrior Mahatma will find no rest until peace and well-being belong to us all.

Resources

◄ **Gandhi**

Most books by Gandhi himself are collections of articles.

Geoffrey Ashe, *Gandhi*, Stein and Day, New York, 1969.
Vinoba Bhave, *Vinoba on Gandhi*, Sarva Seva Sangh, Varanasi, 1973.
Eknath Eswaran, *Gandhi the Man*, Nilgiri Press, Petaluma, California, 1978.
Louis Fischer, *The Life of Mahatma Gandhi*, Collier, New York, 1962. The abridged version is *Gandhi: His Life and Message for the World*, New American Library, New York, 1954.
Mohandas K. Gandhi, *All Men Are Brothers*, Continuum, New York, 1980. Selected passages from the full range of Gandhi's thought.
———, *Nonviolent Resistance*, Schocken, New York, 1967.
———, *An Autobiography: The Story of My Experiments with Truth*, Beacon, Boston, 1957. A selective account, up to the mid-1920s.
———, *Economic and Industrial Relations*, 3 vols., Navajivan, Ahmedabad, 1957.
———, *Basic Education*, Navajivan, Ahmedabad, 1956.
———, *Nonviolence in Peace and War*, 2 vols., Navajivan, Ahmedabad, 1948, 1949.
———, *Hind Swaraj, or Indian Home Rule*, Navajivan, Ahmedabad, 1939.
Richard Gregg, *The Power of Nonviolence*, Schocken, New York, 1966.
Gene Sharp, *Gandhi as a Political Strategist*, Porter Sargent, Boston, 1979.

◄ **Vinoba Bhave**

Vinoba Bhave, *Vinoba on Gandhi*, Sarva Seva Sangh, Varanasi, 1973.
———, *Democratic Values*, Sarva Seva Sangh, Varanasi, 1964. Selected talks on his social philosophy.
(Joseph Jean) Lanza del Vasto, *Gandhi to Vinoba: The New Pilgrimage*, Schocken, New York, 1974. Biography, plus a journal of a Bhoodan tour.

Sriman Narayan, *Vinoba: His Life and Work*, Popular Prakashan, Bombay, 1970.

Vishwanath Tandon, ed., *Selections from Vinoba*, Sarva Seva Sangh, Varanasi, 1981.

Hallam Tennyson, *India's Walking Saint: The Story of Vinoba Bhave*, Doubleday, Garden City, New York, 1955.

◄ Jayaprakash Narayan

Ajit Bhattacharjea, *Jayaprakash Narayan: A Political Biography*, Vikas, New Delhi, 1975.

Jayaprakash Narayan, *The Essential JP*, ed. Satish Kumar, Prism Press, Dorchester, England, 1978. Mostly the *Prison Diary* (see below).

————, *Prison Diary*, University of Washington, Seattle and London, 1977. Written during the Emergency.

Vasant Nargolkar, *JP's Crusade for Total Revolution*, S. Chand, New Delhi, 1975.

◄ Sarvodaya Movement—General

Aside from published sources—most of them listed here, additional ones listed in my booklet *Since Gandhi* (see below)—I drew heavily from two unpublished sources for the historical overview in chapter 2: an early draft of *Nonviolent Revolution in India*, by Geoffrey Ostergaard of the Faculty of Commerce and Social Science, University of Birmingham, England (see listing below); and a paper by Roderick Church of the Department of Politics, Brock University, Ontario, Canada, who is himself working on a full-length study of the movement. I am indebted to them both.

Narayan Desai, *Handbook for Satyagrahis: A Manual for Volunteers of Total Revolution*, Gandhi Peace Foundation, New Delhi, and Movement for a New Society, Philadelphia, 1980.

————, *Towards a Nonviolent Revolution*, Sarva Seva Sangh, Varanasi, 1972. On Shanti Sena.

Erica Linton, *Fragments of a Vision: A Journey through India's Gramdan Villages*, Sarva Seva Sangh, Varanasi, 1971.

Anupam Mishra and Satyendra Tripathi, *The Chipko Movement*, People's Action (Gandhi Peace Foundation), New Delhi, 1978.

Geoffrey Ostergaard, *Nonviolent Revolution in India*, JP Amrit Kosh, Sevagram, and Gandhi Peace Foundation, New Delhi, 1985. By far, the most extensive treatment of Sarvodaya history available. Emphasizes the period of Jayaprakash Narayan's dominance, to the present.

Mark Shepard, *Since Gandhi: India's Sarvodaya Movement*, Greenleaf, Weare, New Hampshire, 1984. Booklet, mimeographed. Similar to the account of Sarvodaya history in chapter 2, but more detailed and critical, with an alternative viewpoint to Ostergaard's.

◄ Other Lands

Robert Cooney and Helen Michaelowski, *The Power of the People: Active Nonviolence in the United States*, Peace Press, Los Angeles, 1977. A historical overview.

Virginia Coover et al., *Resource Manual for a Living Revolution*, New Society Press, Philadelphia, 1977. A handbook compiled by Movement for a New Society.

James H. Forest, *The Unified Buddhist Church of Vietnam: Fifteen Years for Reconciliation*, International Fellowship of Reconciliation, Alkmaar, Netherlands, 1978.

A. Paul Hare and Herb Blumberg, eds., *Liberation without Violence*, Rex Collings, London, 1977. Includes "peace brigade" actions by Shanti Sena, the World Peace Brigade, the Cyprus Resettlement Project, and others.

Marjorie Hope and James Young, *The Struggle for Humanity: Agents of Nonviolent Change in a Violent World*, Orbis, Maryknoll, New York, 1977. Includes chapters on Movement for a New Society, Lanza del Vasto, Danilo Dolci, Dom Helder Camara, Cesar Chavez, the Unified Buddhist Church, and Kenneth Kaunda. Highly recommended.

Institute for Community Economics, *The Community Land Trust Handbook*, Rodale Press, Emmaus, Pennsylvania, 1982.

Detlef Kantowsky, *Sarvodaya: The Other Development*, Vikas, New Delhi, 1980. A scholarly view of both the Indian movement and Sarvodaya Shramadana of Sri Lanka.

(Joseph Jean) Lanza del Vasto, *Warriors of Peace: Writings on the Technique of Nonviolence*, Knopf, New York, 1974. Mostly accounts of the Ark's campaigns.

————, *Return to the Source*, Schocken, New York, 1972. Includes an account of the author's visit with Gandhi.

Jacques Levy, *Cesar Chavez: Autobiography of La Causa*, Norton, New York, 1975.

Joanna Macy, *Dharma and Development*, Kumarion, West Hartford, Connecticut, 1983. On Sarvodaya Shramadana of Sri Lanka.

Jerry Mangione, *The World around Danilo Dolci: A Passion for Sicilians*, Harper and Row, New York, 1972.

George McRobie, *Small Is Possible*, Harper and Row, New York, 1981. On the Intermediate Technology Development Group.

John Mercer, *The Spinner's Workshop: A Social History and Practical Guide*, Prism Press, Dorchester, England, 1978. A Gandhian approach.

Michael N. Nagler, *America without Violence: Why Violence Persists and How You Can Stop It*, Island Press, Covelo, California, 1982. An excellent introduction to principles of nonviolence.

E. F. Schumacher, *Small Is Beautiful: Economics as If People Mattered*, Harper and Row, New York, 1973.

Gene Sharp, *The Politics of Nonviolent Action*, 3 vols., Porter Sargent, Boston, 1973. A comprehensive review and analysis of methods and historical examples.

————, *Making Europe Unconquerable: The Potential of Civilian-Based Deterrence and Defence*, Francis, London, and Ballinger, Cambridge, Massachusetts, 1985.

Mark Shepard, "Island of Peace: The Community of the Ark," *Fellowship*, June 1981, pp. 3–6.

◄ Magazines

The following regularly deal with Gandhian thought and/or action in their respective countries and worldwide.

The Acorn, Philosophy Department, Eastern Illinois University, Charleston, Illinois 61920, USA. Scholarly; biannual.

Catholic Worker, 36 East First Street, New York, New York 10003, USA. Organ of the Catholic Worker movement (Christian/Gandhian nonviolence, decentralism, service); monthly.

Fellowship, Box 271, Nyack, New York 10960, USA. Journal of the Fellowship of Reconciliation; monthly.

MANAS, Box 32112, Los Angeles, California 90032, USA. Philosophical and decentralist review; weekly.

Peace News, 8 Elm Avenue, Nottingham, England. Secular, leftist; biweekly.

Resurgence, Ford House, Hartland, Bideford, Devon, England. Decentralist; monthly.

India

The following Gandhian magazines from India are in English.

Gandhi Marg, 221 Deen Dayal Upadhyaya Marg, New Delhi 110 002. Scholarly journal of the Gandhi Peace Foundation; monthly.
Gandhi Vigyan, 2-2-1133/5/5 New Nallakunta, Hyderabad 500 044. Scholarly journal of the Gandhi Institute of Studies; monthly.
Science for Villages, Center of Science for Villages, Magan Sangrahalaya, Wardha, Maharashtra 442 001. Monthly.
Vigil, Bakharabad, Cuttack 753 002. Organ of Sarva Seva Sangh; weekly.

◄ Addresses

Addresses marked with an asterisk (*) are sources for books listed above. Most of the organizations listed appreciate donations.

India

Letters to India can be in English, but the envelope should be addressed in capital letters. Send by airmail for reasonable delivery times.

Agrindus Institute
Govindpur
Mirzapur Dt.
Uttar Pradesh 231 221

Bombay Sarvodaya Friendship
    Centre
c/o Daniel Mazgaonkar
Shanti Kutir
Navghar Road
Mulund East
Bombay 400 081
(Provides hospitality and guidance to foreigners interested in the Gandhian movement.)

Brahma Vidya Mandir
Parandham
Paunar
Wardha
Maharashtra 442 001
(Vinoba's ashram.)

Narayan Desai
Institute for Total Revolution
Vedchhi
Surat Dt.
Gujarat 394 641

*Gandhi Book House
1 Rajghat Colony
New Delhi 110 002

Gandhi Peace Foundation
221 Deen Dayal Upadhyaya
    Marg
New Delhi 110 002
(Promotes Gandhian thought and action, aids serious foreign inquirers, maintains a hostel. Address inquiries on the Chipko Movement here, to Anupam Mishra.)

Radhakrishna Menon
P.O. Pudukode
(via Ramnatkara)
Calicut
Kerala 673 633

*Navajivan Publishing House
Navajivan Trust
Post Navajivan
Ahmedabad
Gujarat 380 014

Harivallabh Parikh
Anand Niketan
Rangpur (via Kosindra)
Baroda Dt.
Gujarat 391 140

*Sarva Seva Sangh
Rajghat
Varanasi
Uttar Pradesh 221 001
(For publications, address "Sarva
Seva Sangh Prakashan.")

Shanti Sena
(Same as Sarva Seva Sangh.)

United States

For United States headquarters of
international organizations, see
"International and Other," below.

Consortium on Peace Research,
   Education And Development
   (COPRED)
University of Illinois at Urbana-
   Champaign
911 West High Street,
   Room 100
Urbana, Illinois 61801

*Fellowship of Reconciliation
Box 271
Nyack, New York 10960

Grassroots Citizen Dispute
   Resolution Clearinghouse
c/o Paul and Priscilla Wahraftig
7514 Kensington Street
Pittsburgh, Pennsylvania 15221
(Information on a United States
movement for people's courts.)

*Greenleaf Books/Friends of the
   Ark
Weare, New Hampshire 03281
(Comprehensive selection of
books on Gandhi and Sarvodaya,
including Indian publications,
plus books by Lanza del Vasto.)

Institute for Community
   Economics
151 Montague City Road
Greenfield, Massachusetts 01301
(Information on land trusts.)

Martin Luther King Center for
   Social Change
449 Auburn Avenue N.E.
Atlanta, Georgia 30312
(A training center.)

Carl Kline
UMHE
802 11th Avenue
Brookings, South Dakota 57006
(Summer study tours to Sarvo-
daya centers.)

*Resource Center for
   Nonviolence
P.O. Box 2324
Santa Cruz, California 95063
(Fellowship of Reconciliation
affiliate. Has bookstore and
library.)

United Farm Workers of America
(UFW)
P.O. Box 62
Keene, California 93570

*War Resisters League
339 Lafayette Street
New York, New York 10012

Witness for Peace
515 Broadway
Santa Cruz, California 95060

England

Fellowship of Reconciliation
9 Coombe Road
New Malden, Surrey KT3 4QA

*Housmans Bookshop
5 Caledonian Road
King's Cross
London N1 9DX

Intermediate Technology
Development Group
9 King Street
London WC2E 8HN

*E. F. Schumacher Society
Ford House
Hartland
Bideford, Devon

International and Other

La Communauté de l'Arche
(The Community of the Ark)
34.260 le Bousquet d'Orb
FRANCE

Danilo Dolci
Centro Studi e Iniziative
Largo Scalla 5
Partinico, Sicily 94047
ITALY

International Fellowship of
Reconciliation
Hof von Sonoy
1811 LD Alkmaar
THE NETHERLANDS

International Peace Research
Association
c/o Chadwick Alger
Mershon Center
Ohio State University
199 West 10th Avenue
Columbus, Ohio 43201
USA

Nonviolent Alternatives
Kerkstraat 150
B 2000 Antwerpen
BELGIUM

Peace Brigades International
4722 Baltimore Avenue
Philadelphia, Pennsylvania 19143
USA

Sarvodaya Shramadana
Movement
77 De Soysa Road
Moratuwa
SRI LANKA

Servicio Paz y Justicia
Mexico 479
(1097) Buenos Aires
ARGENTINA

War Resisters International
55 Dawes Street
London SE17 1EL
ENGLAND

Index